Infinite Love

Melanin Love Stories to Color

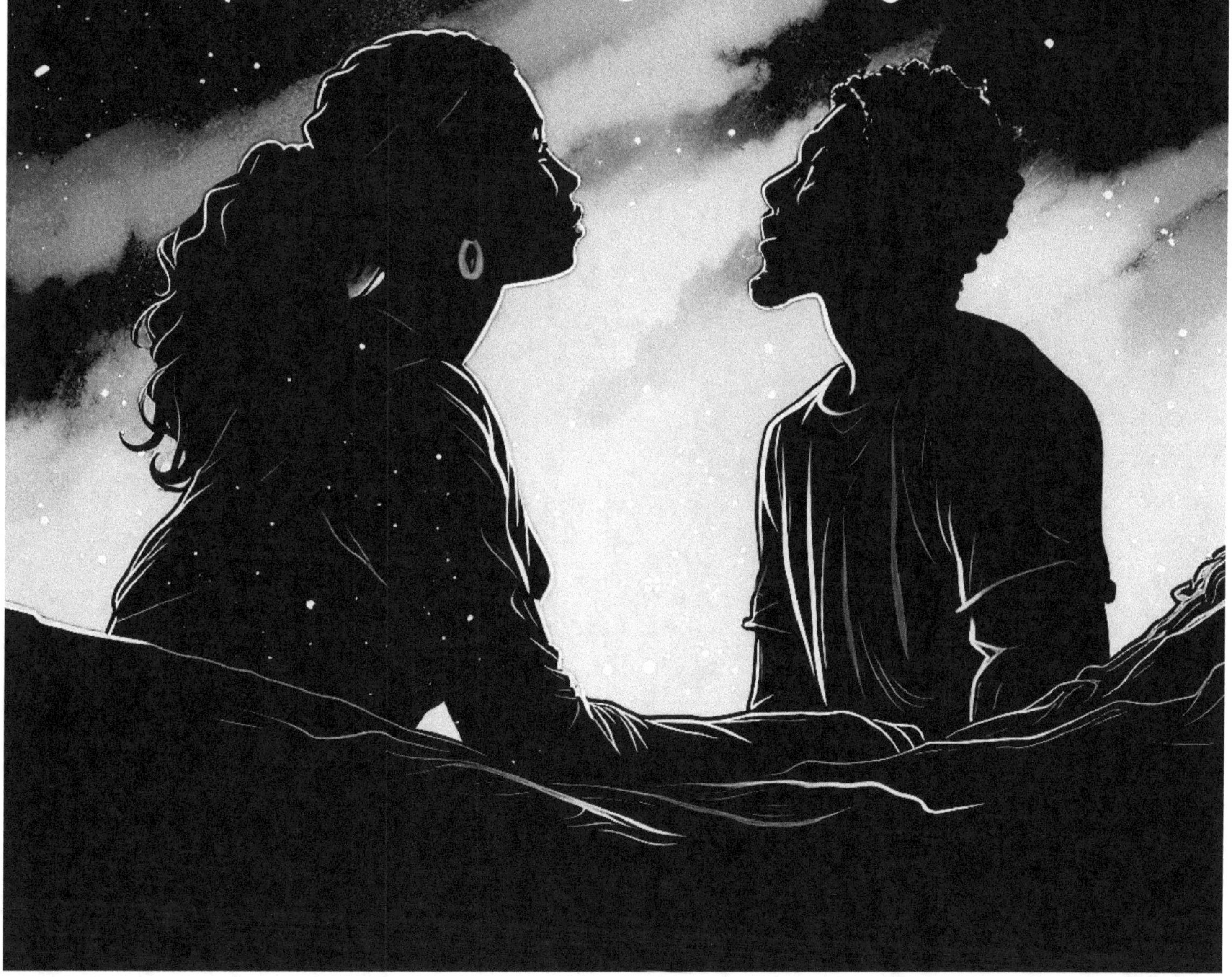

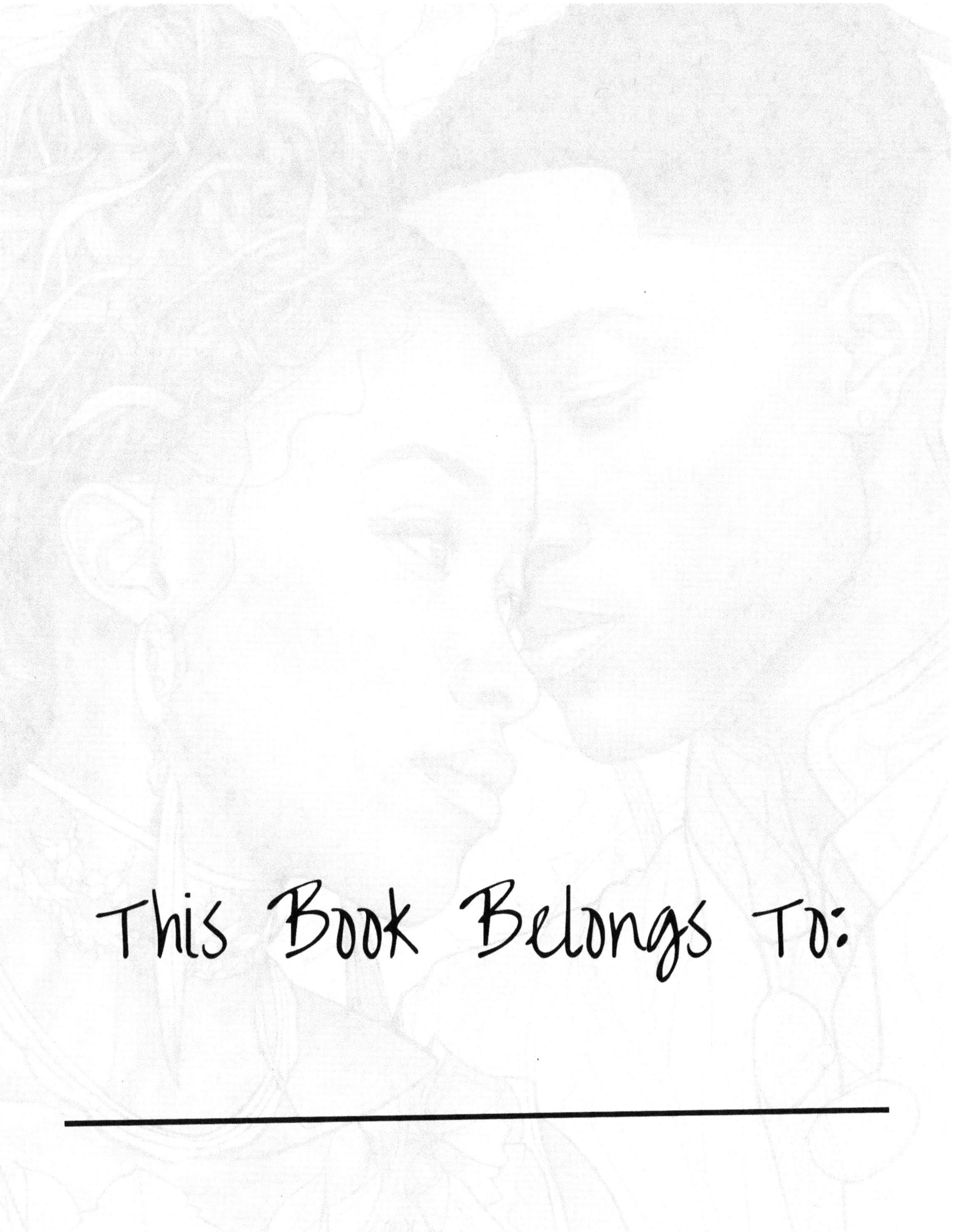

This Book Belongs To:

____

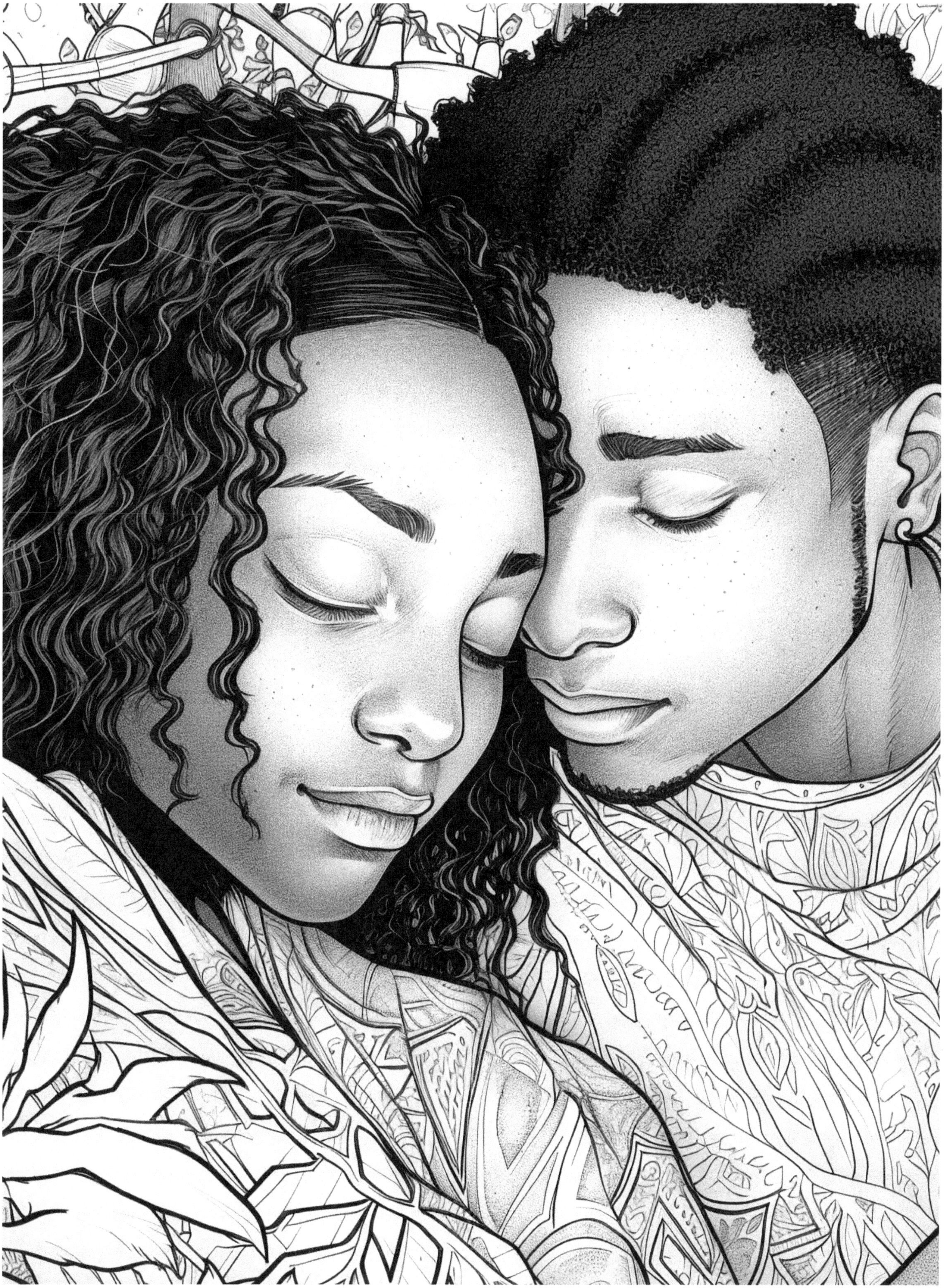

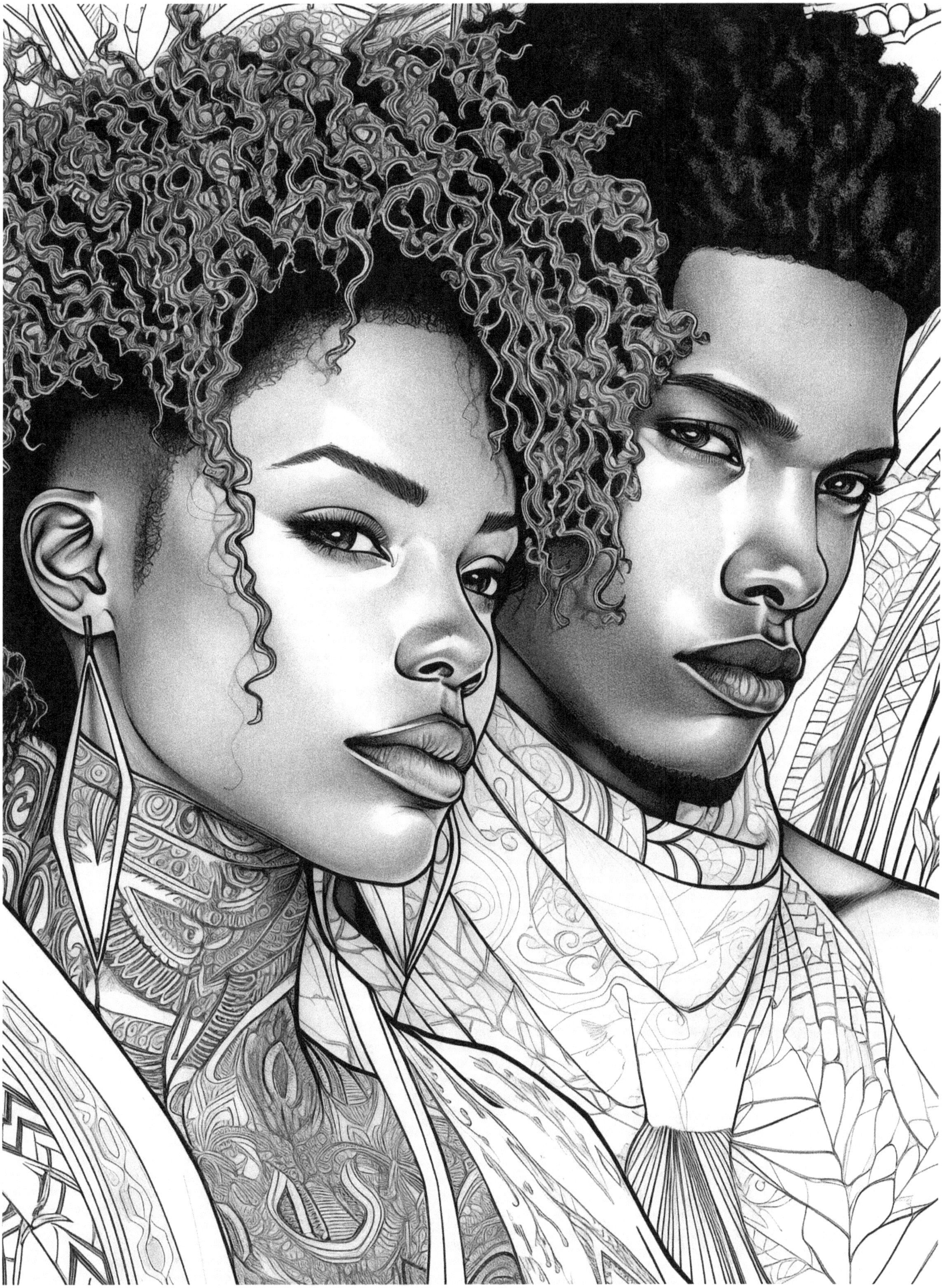

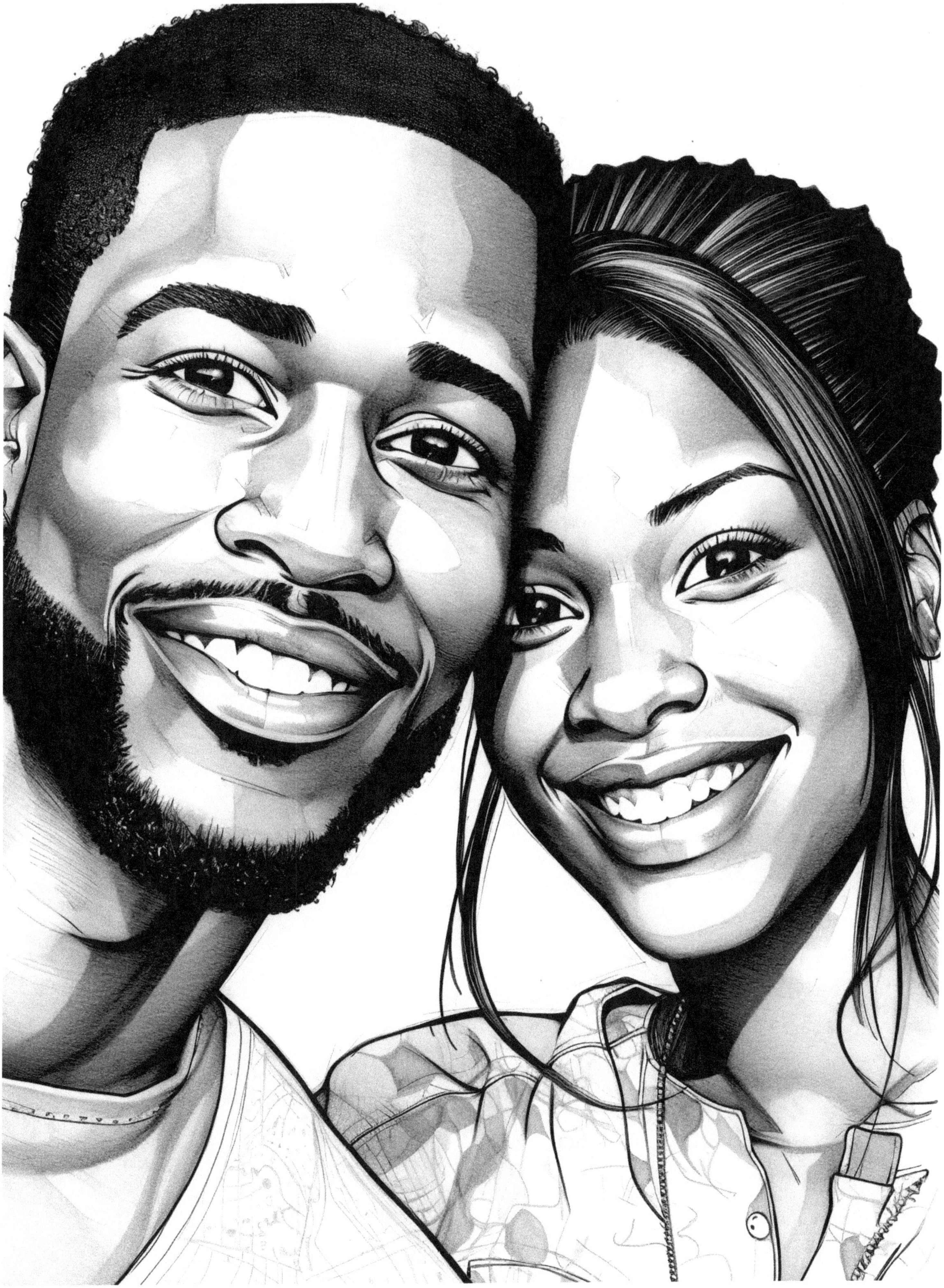

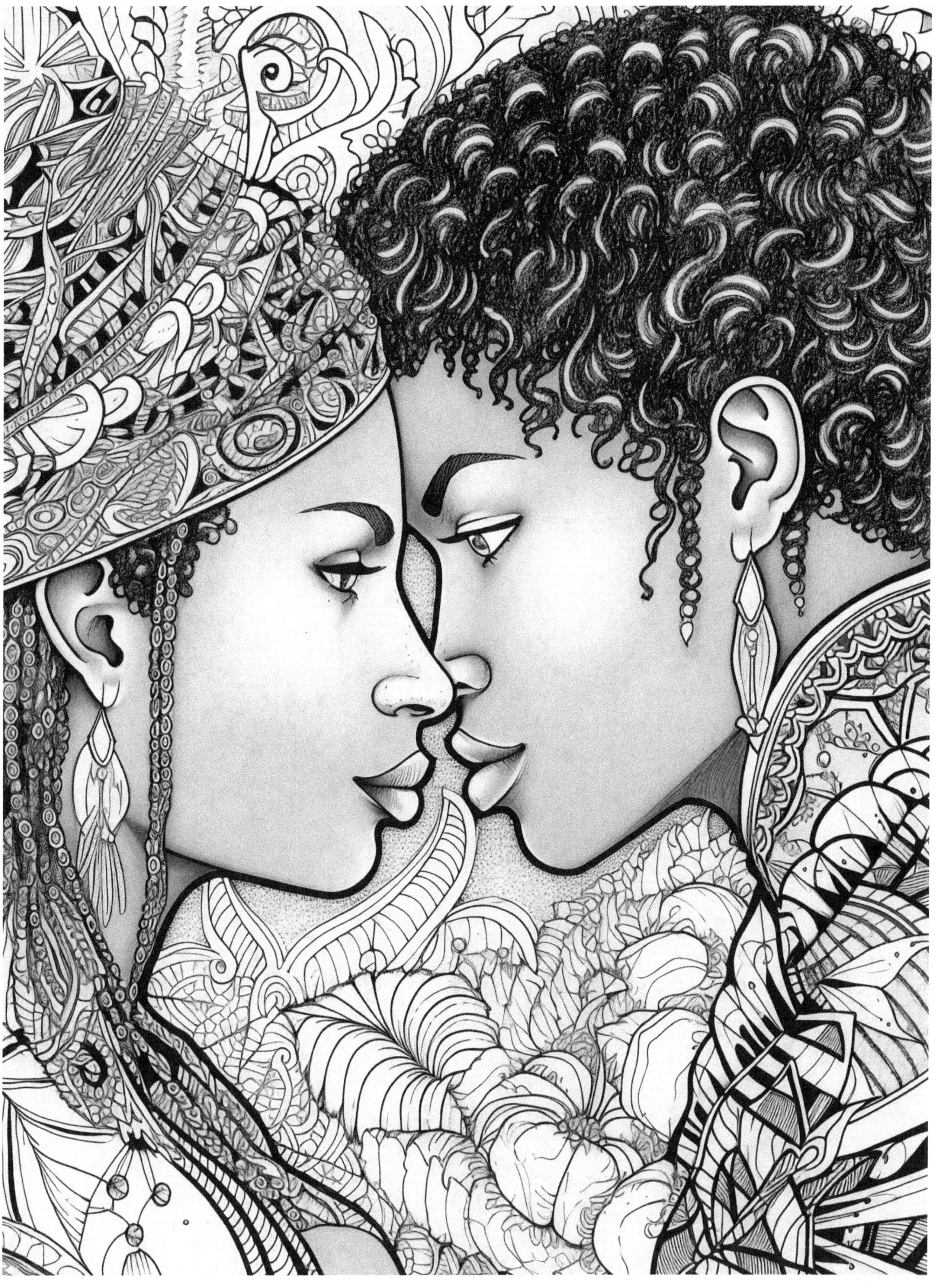

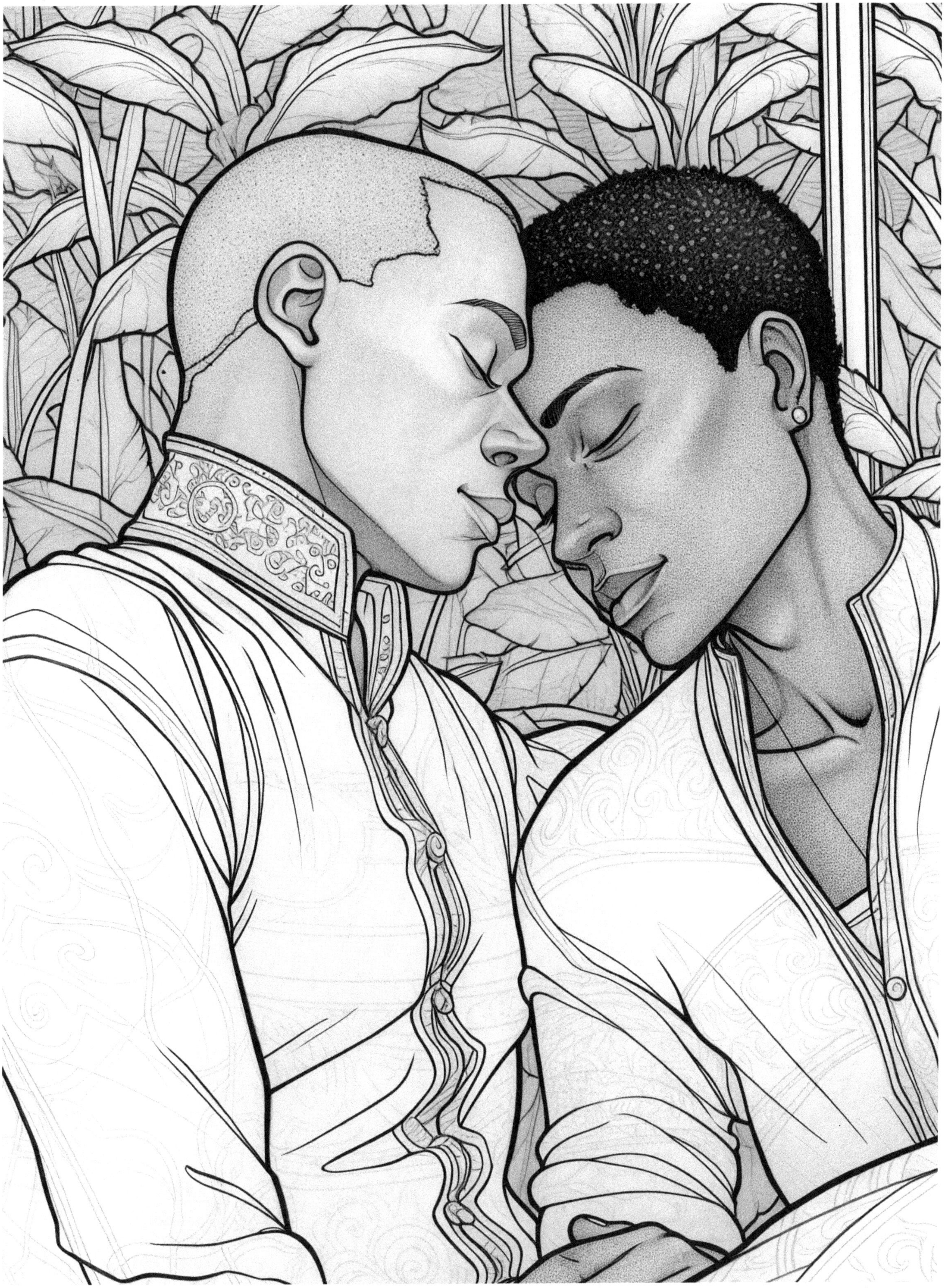

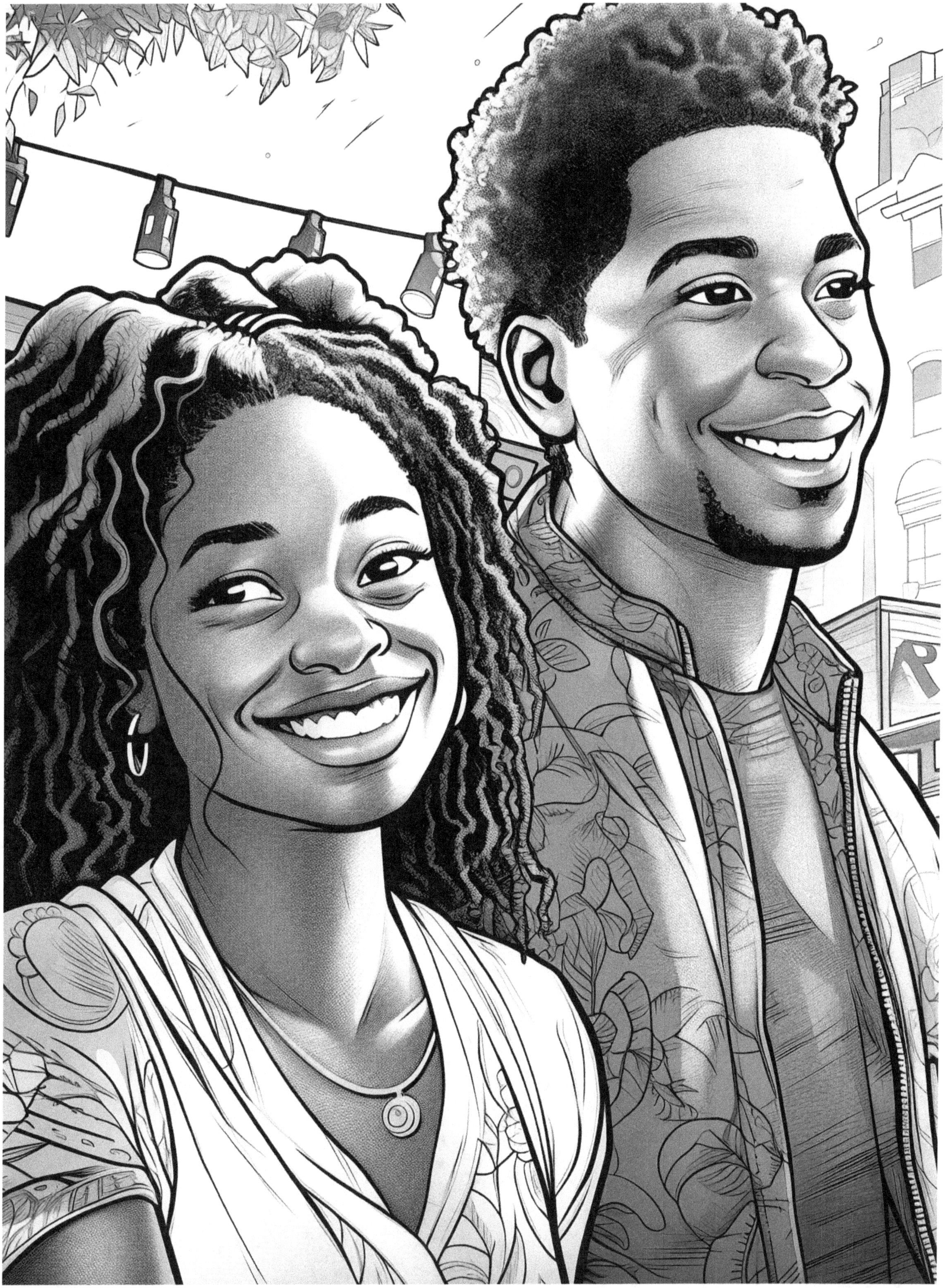

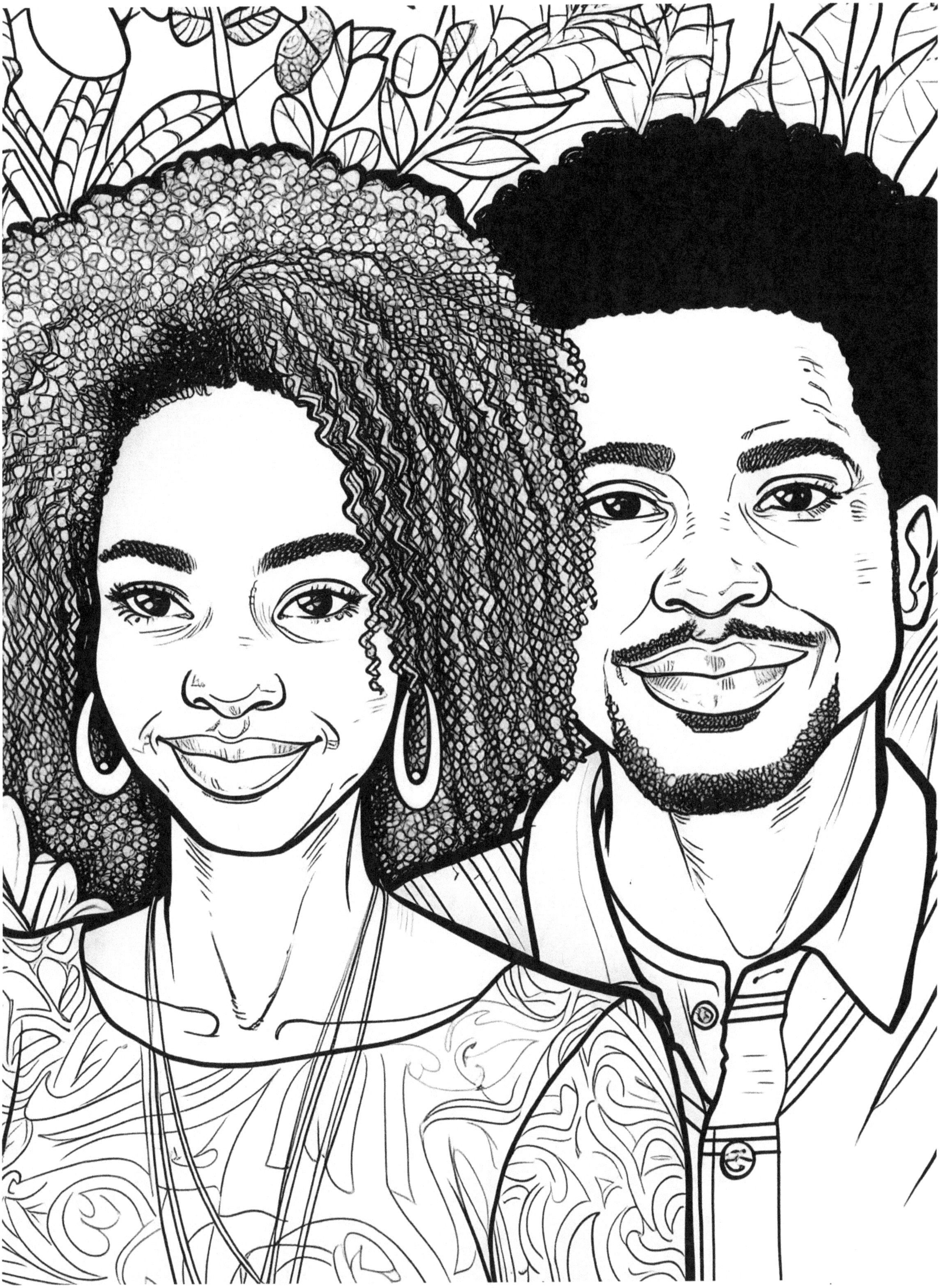

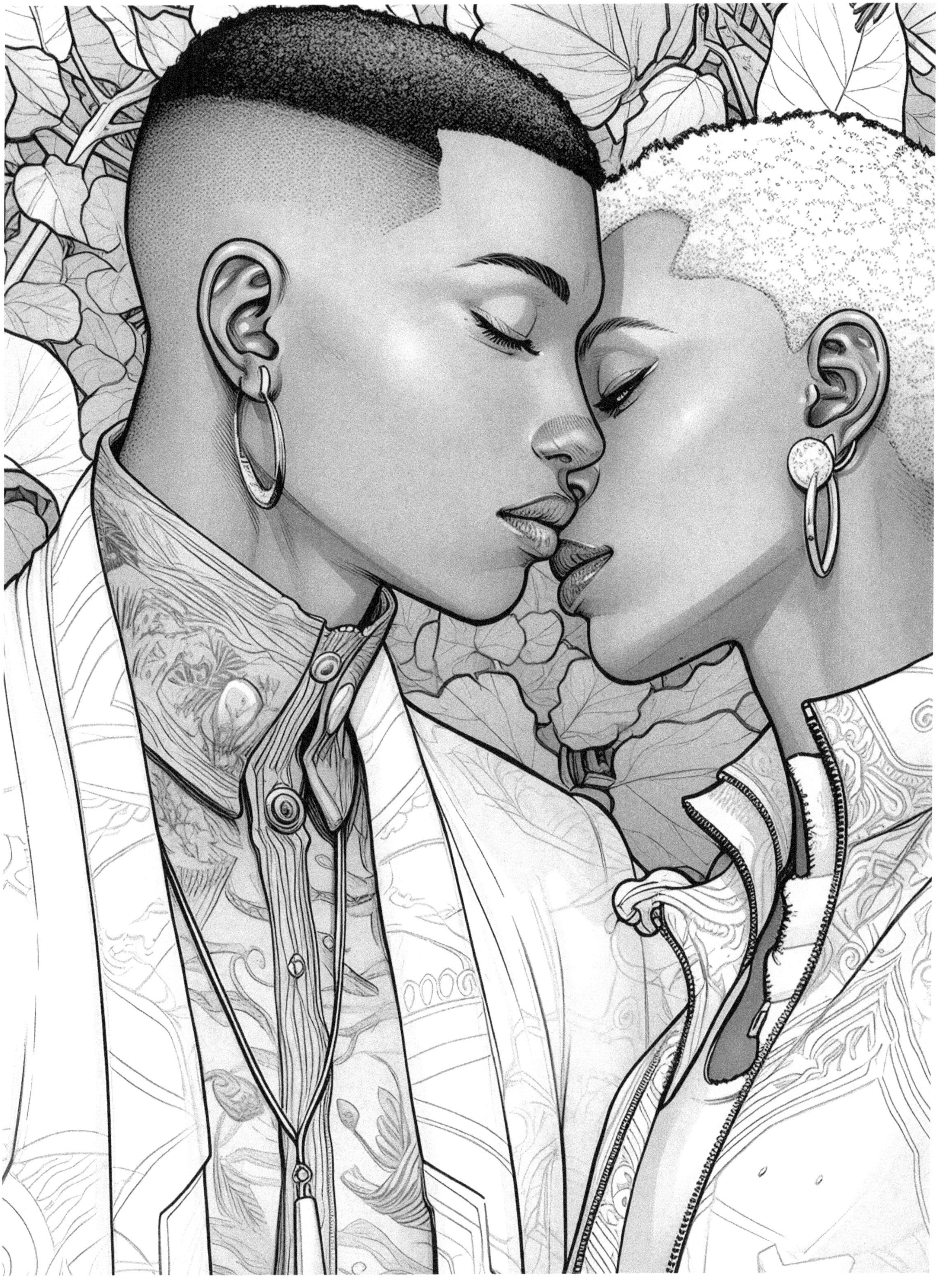

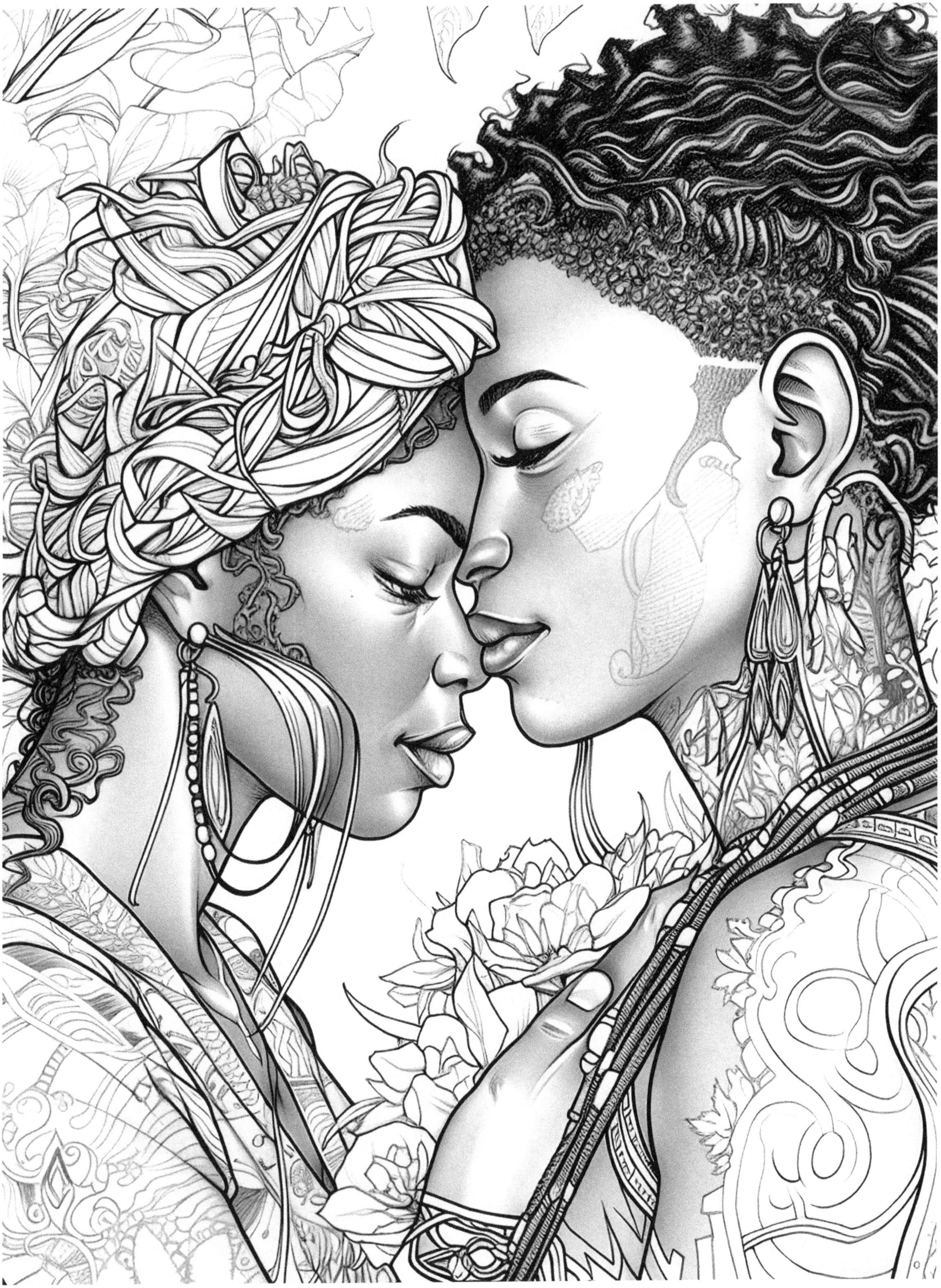

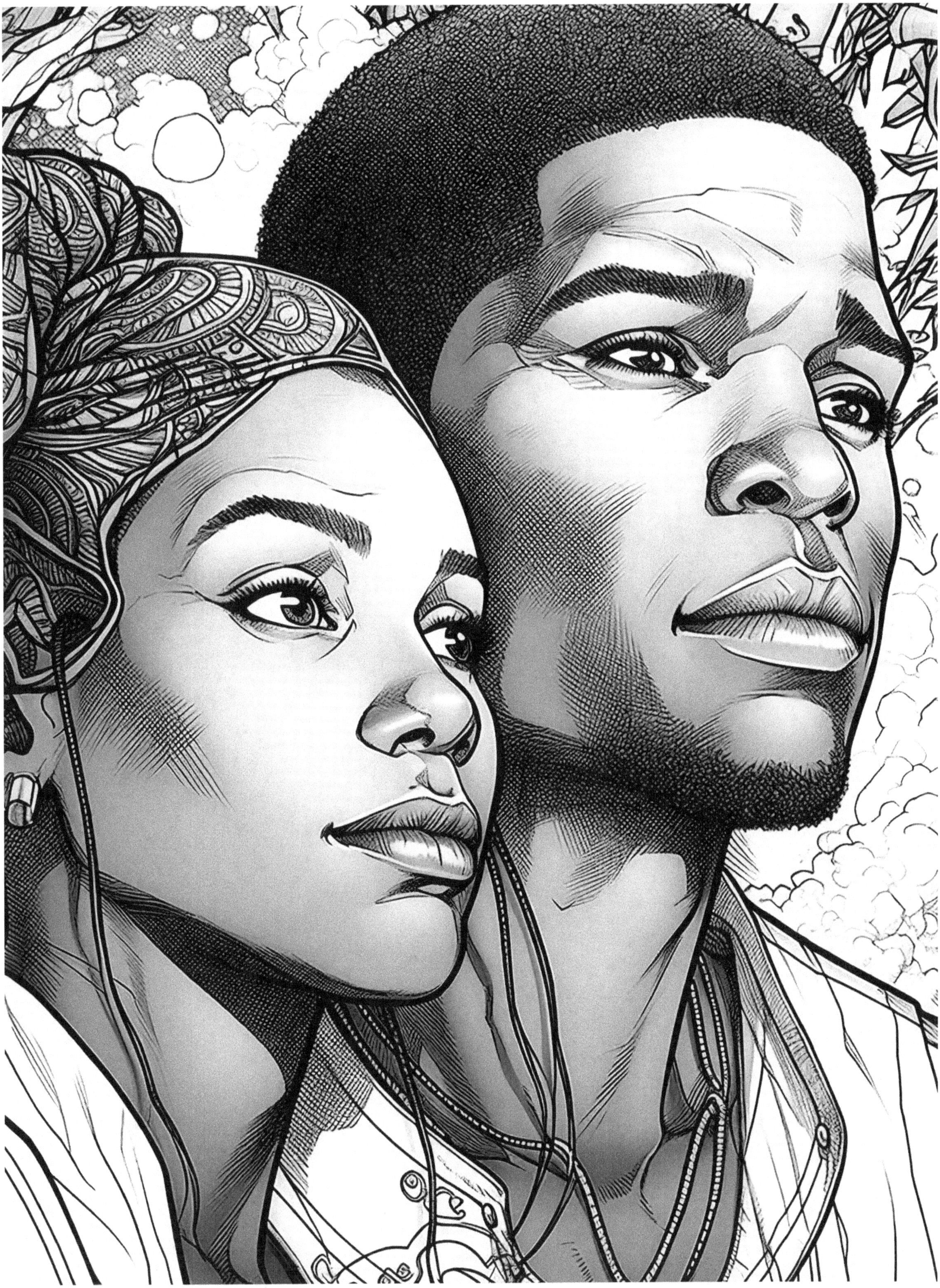

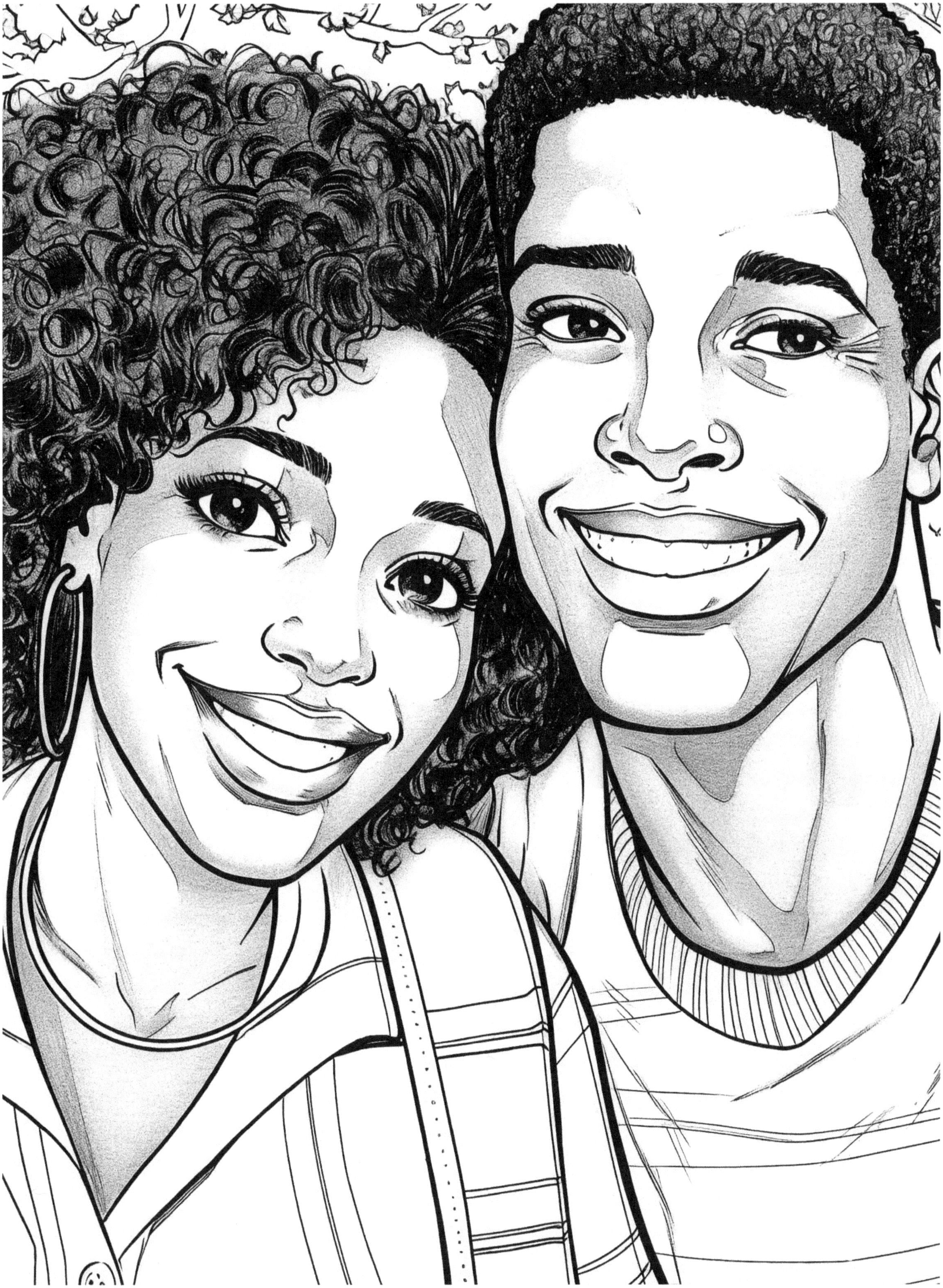

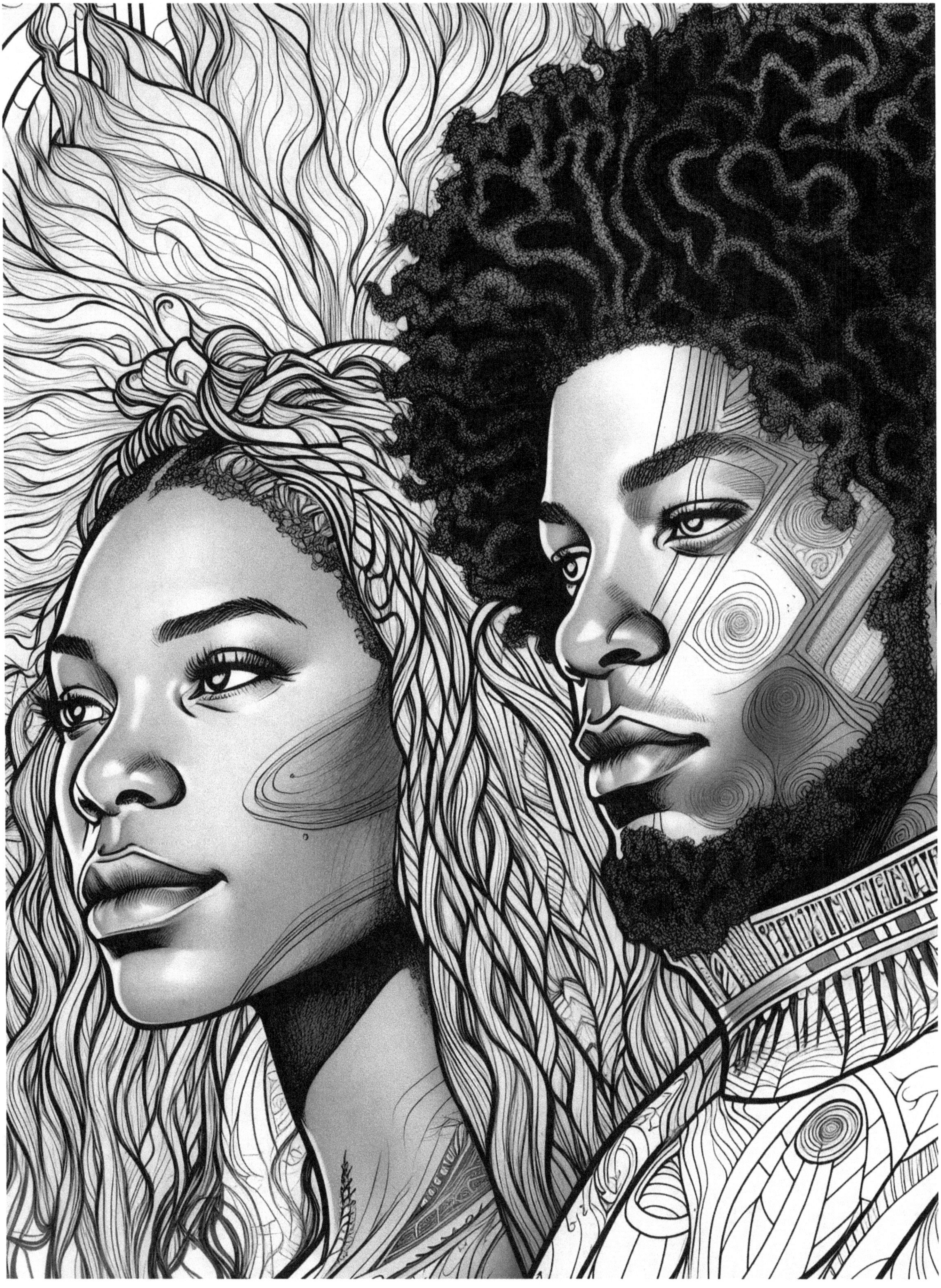

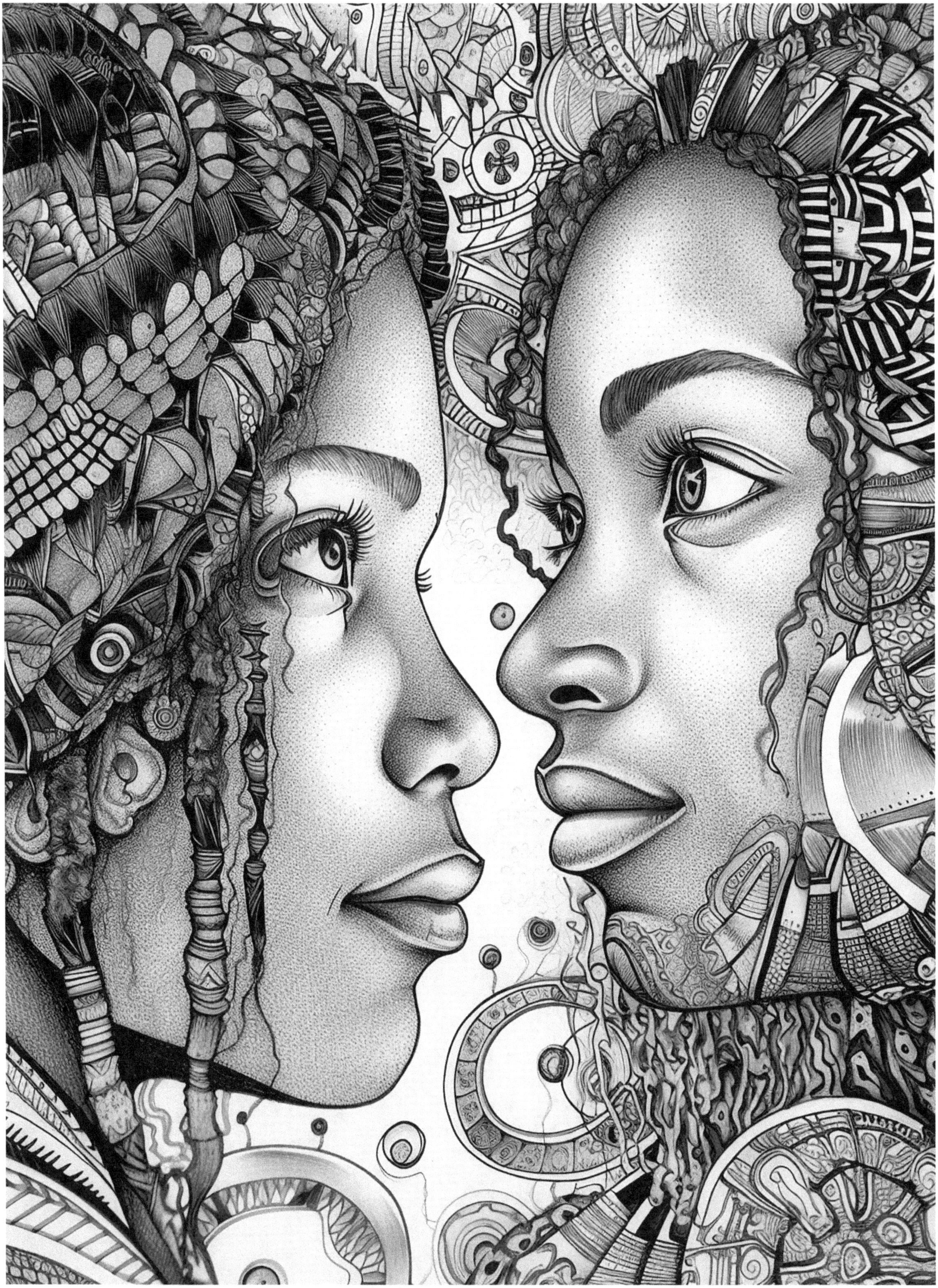

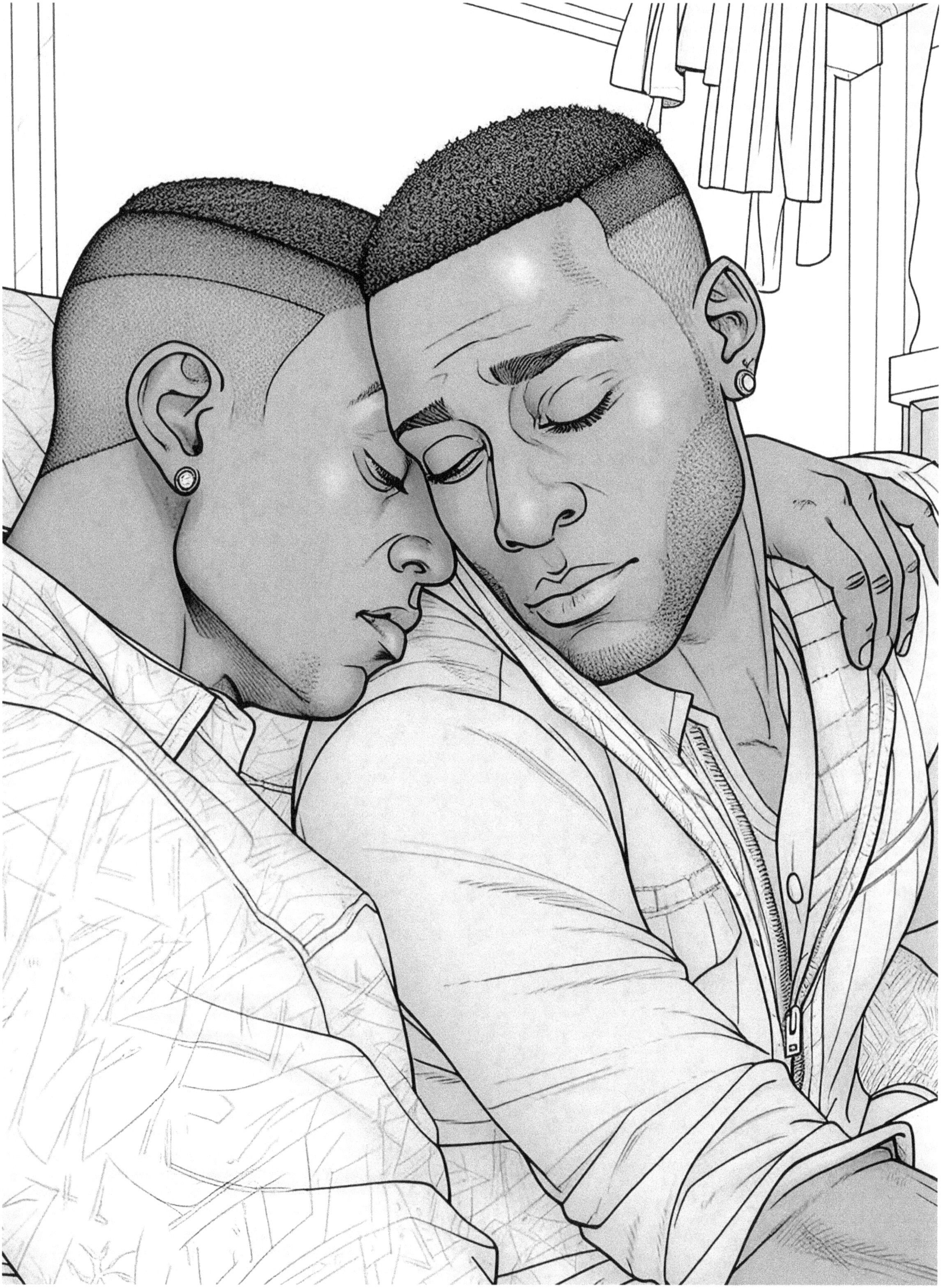

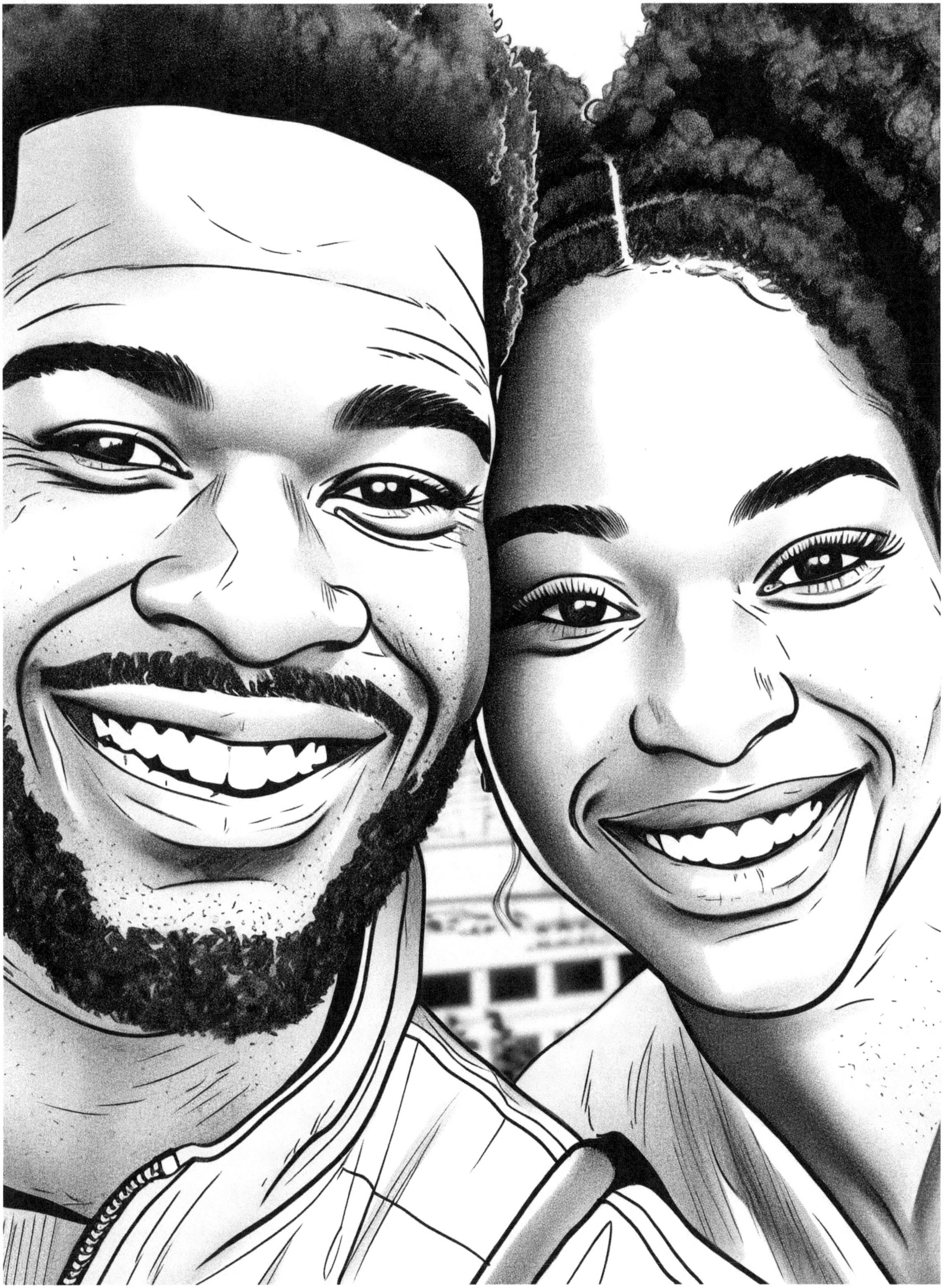

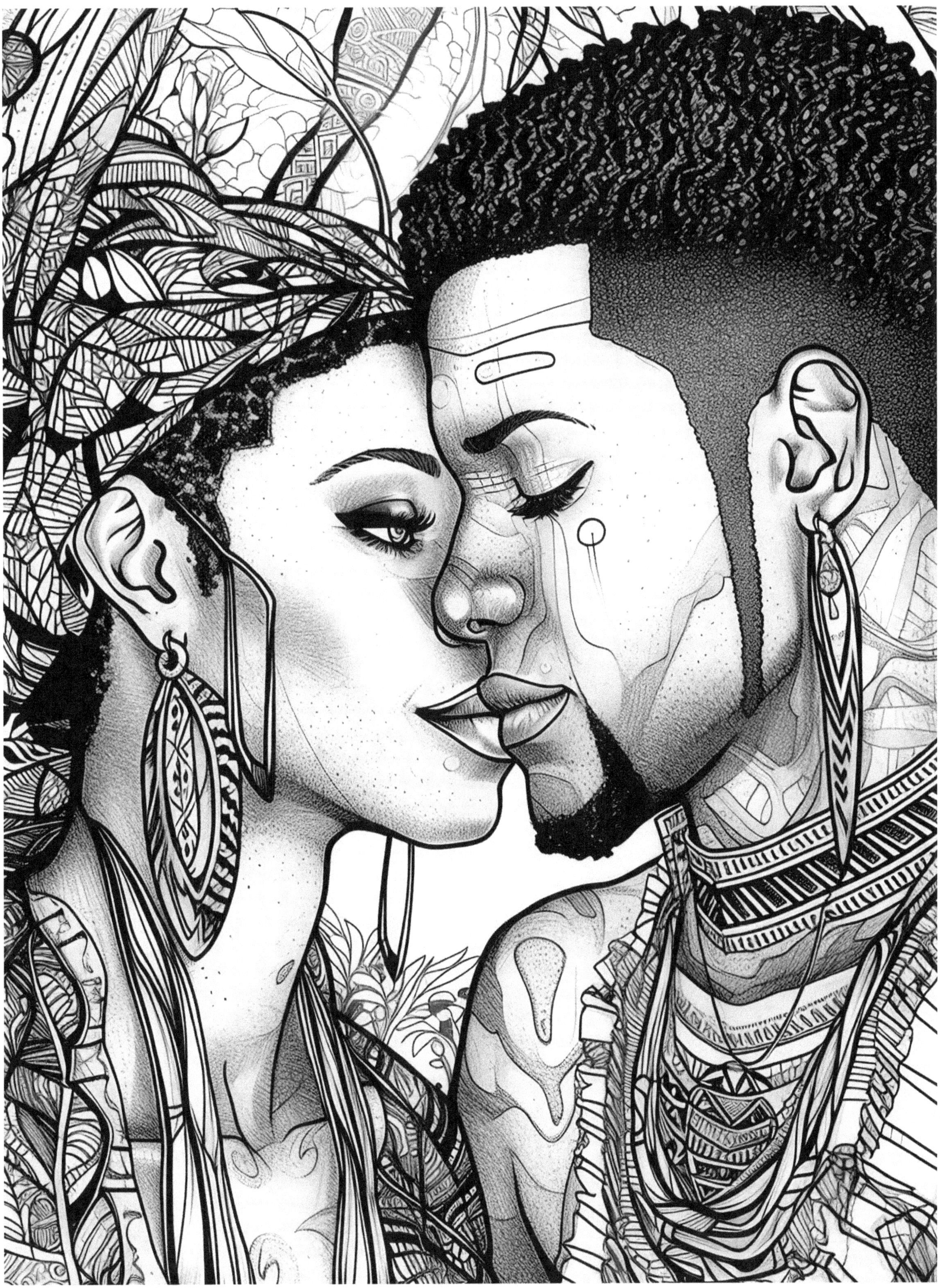

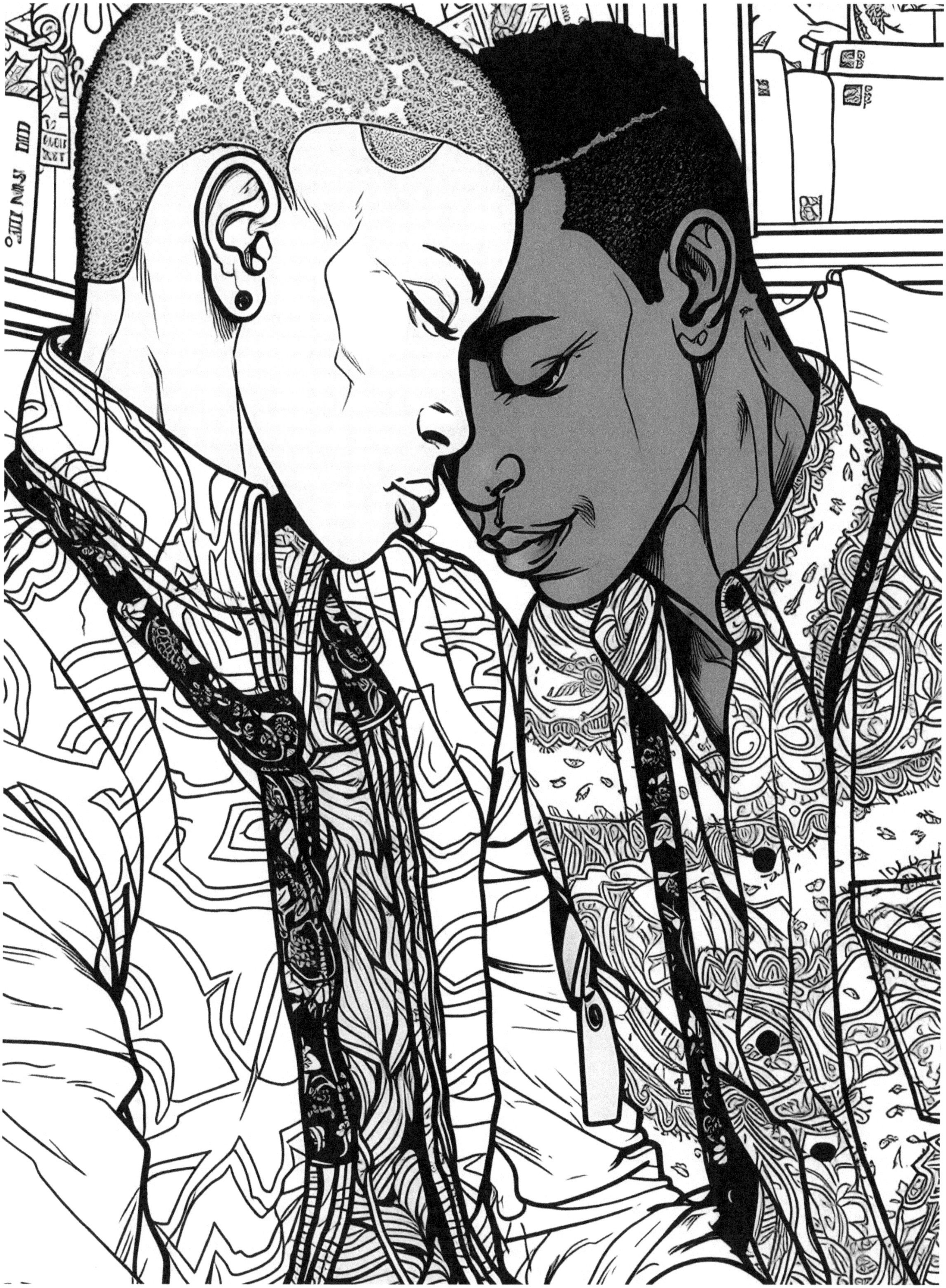

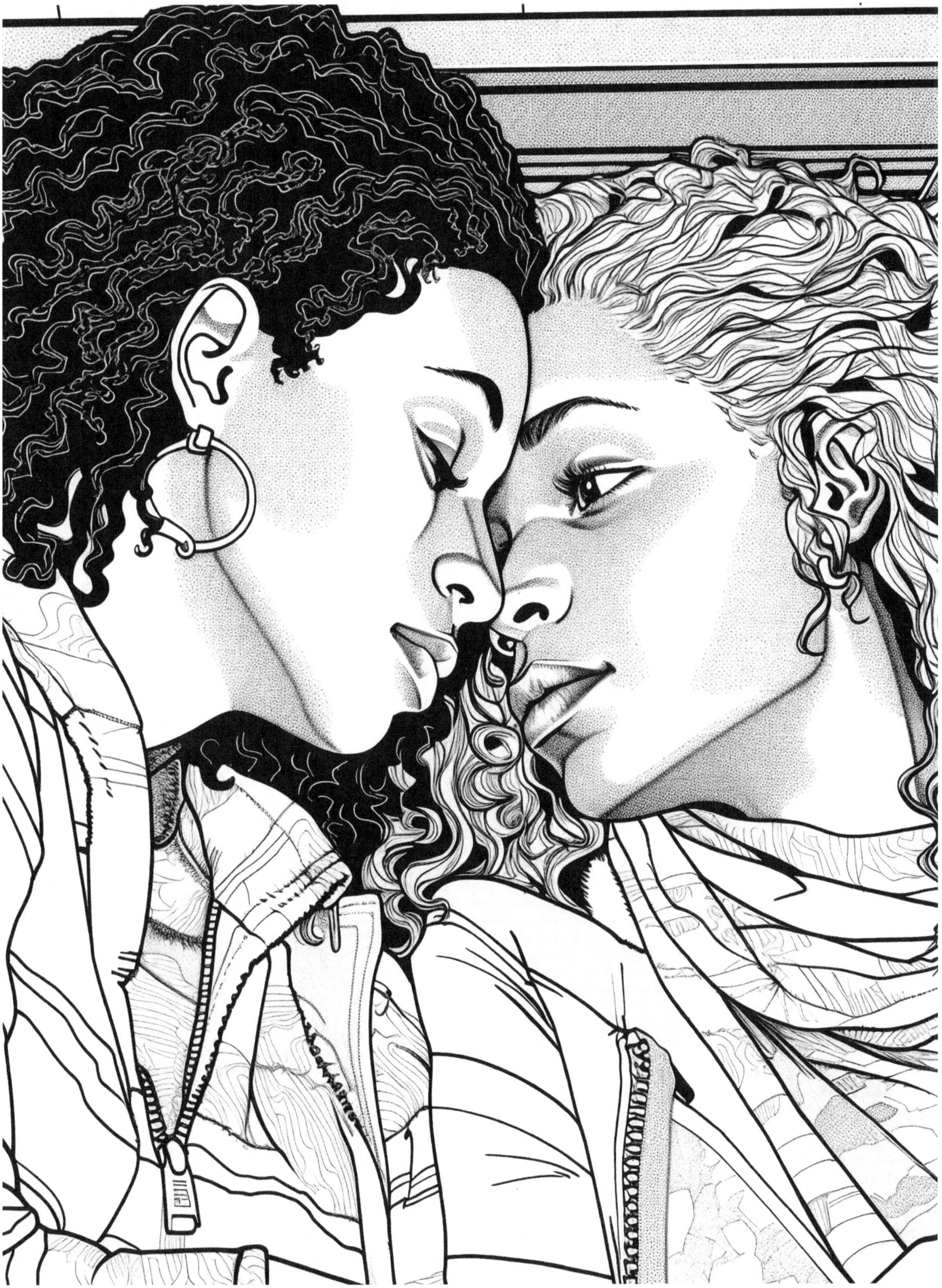

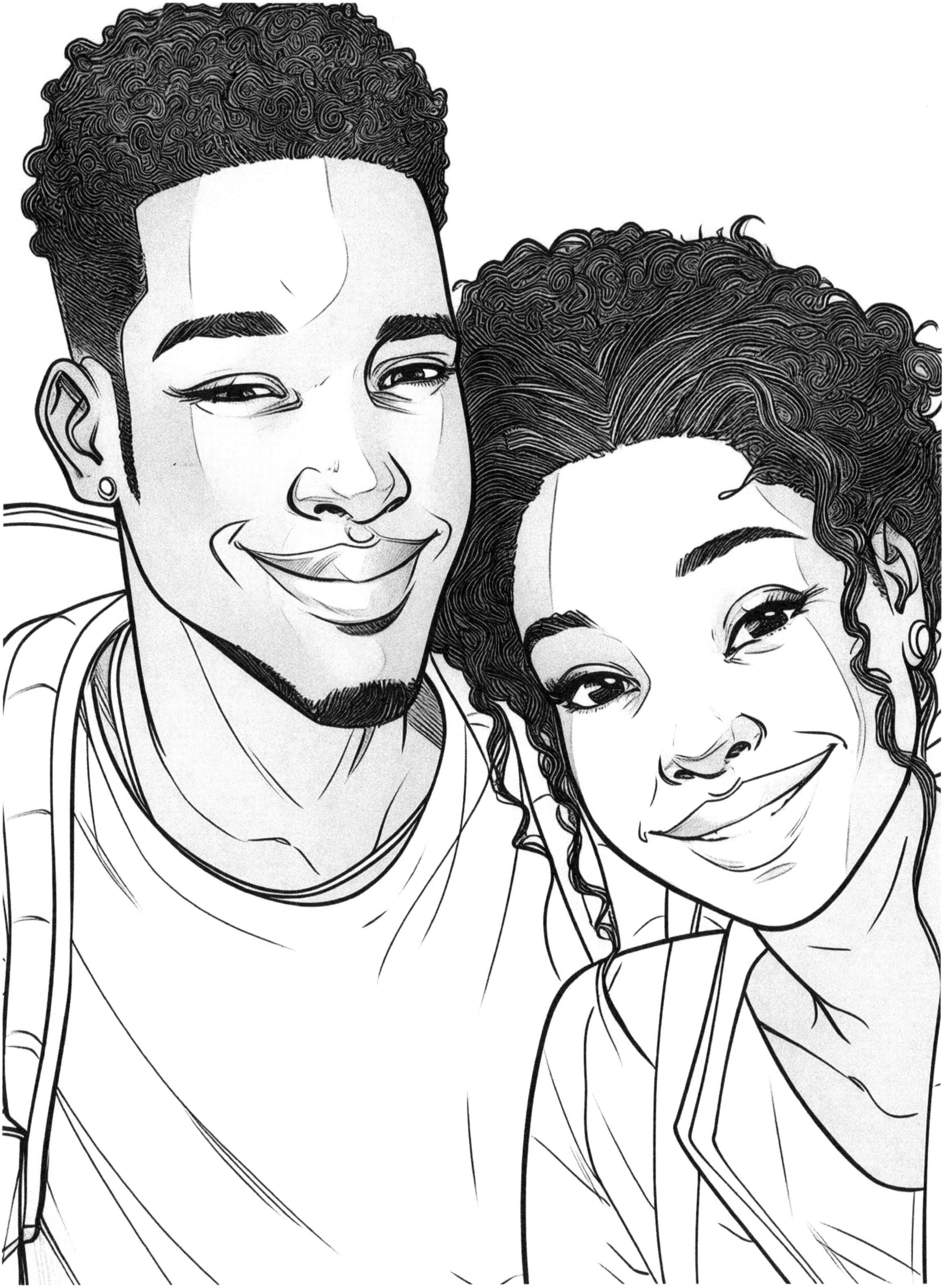

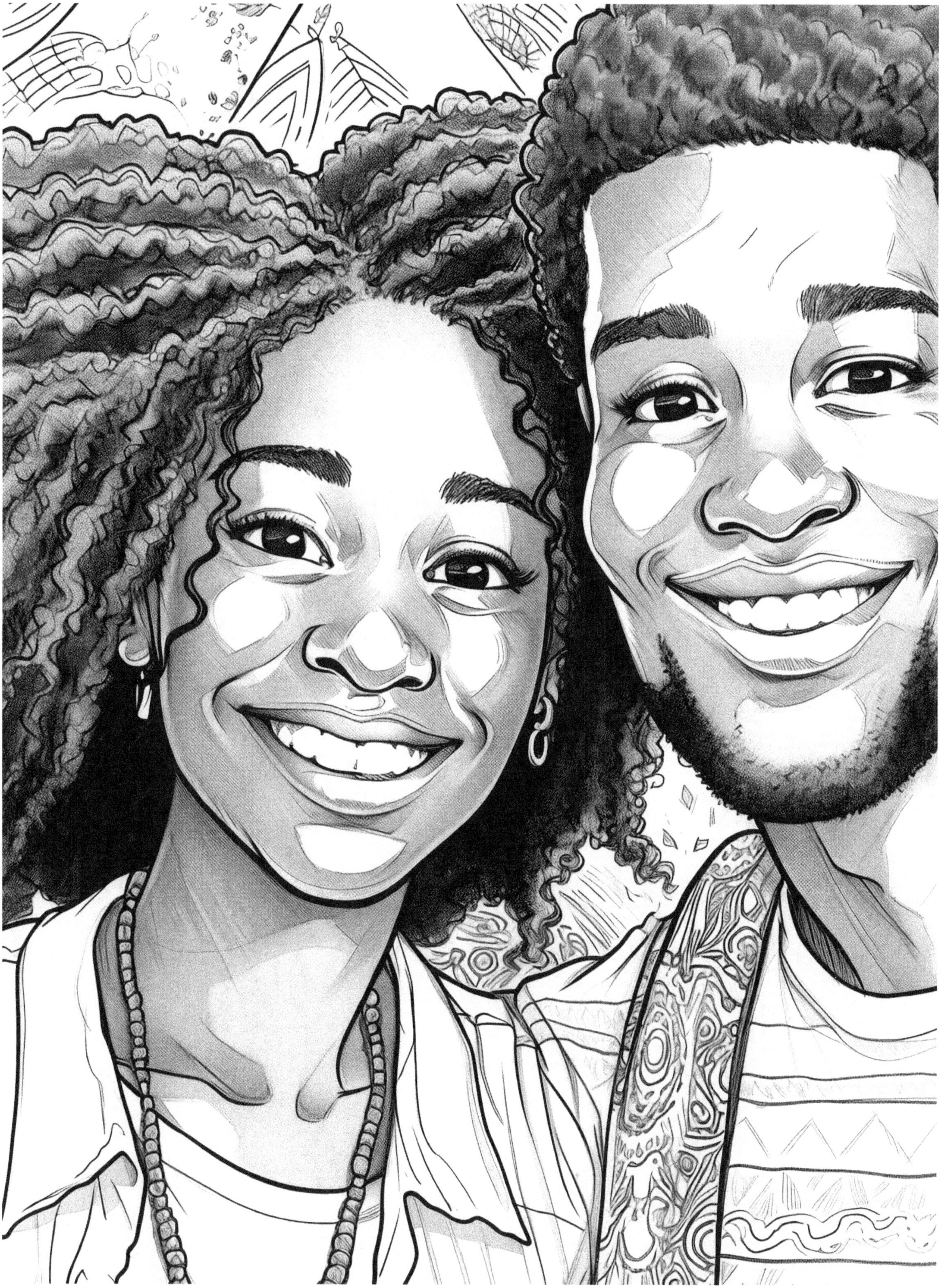

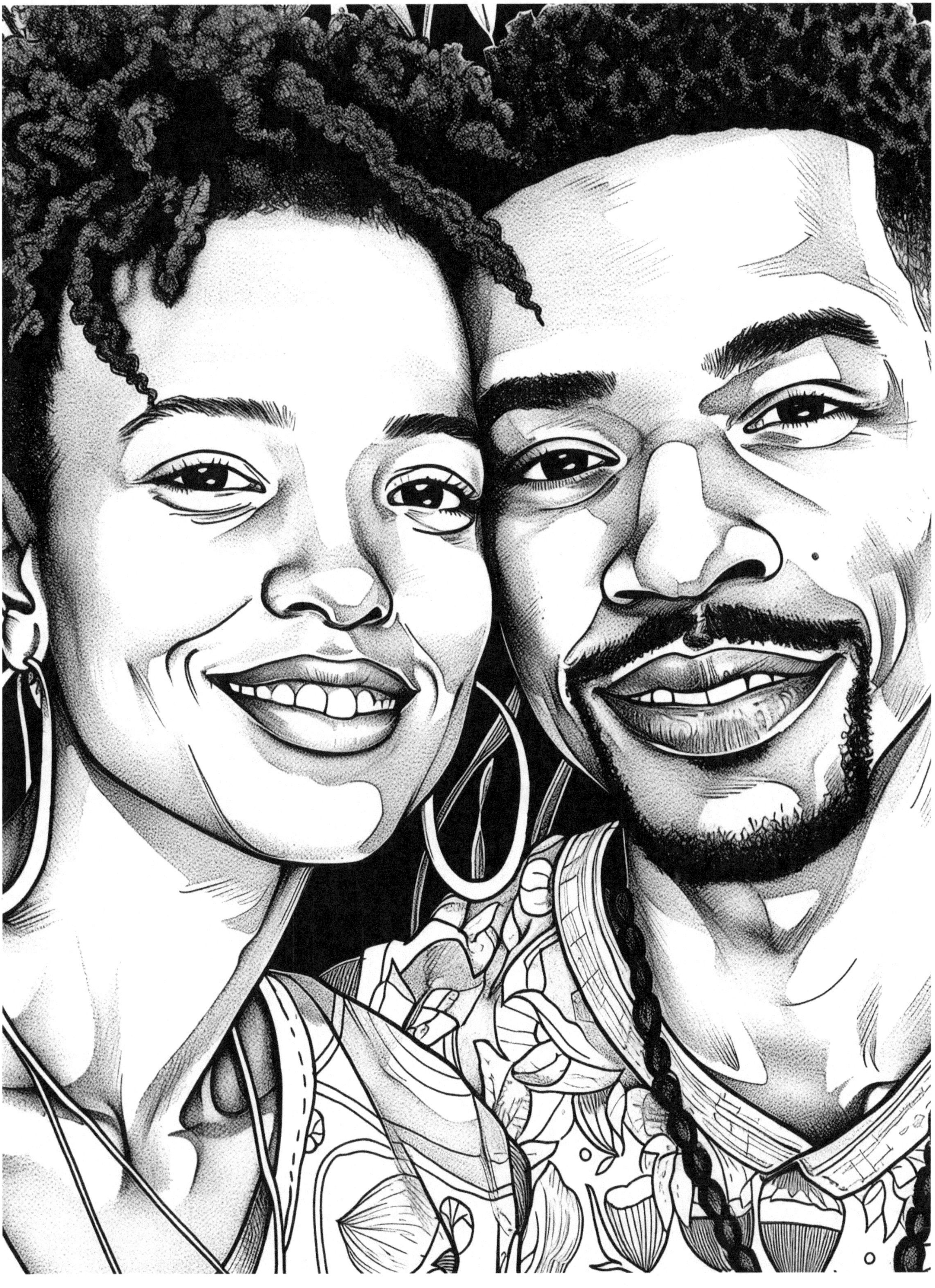

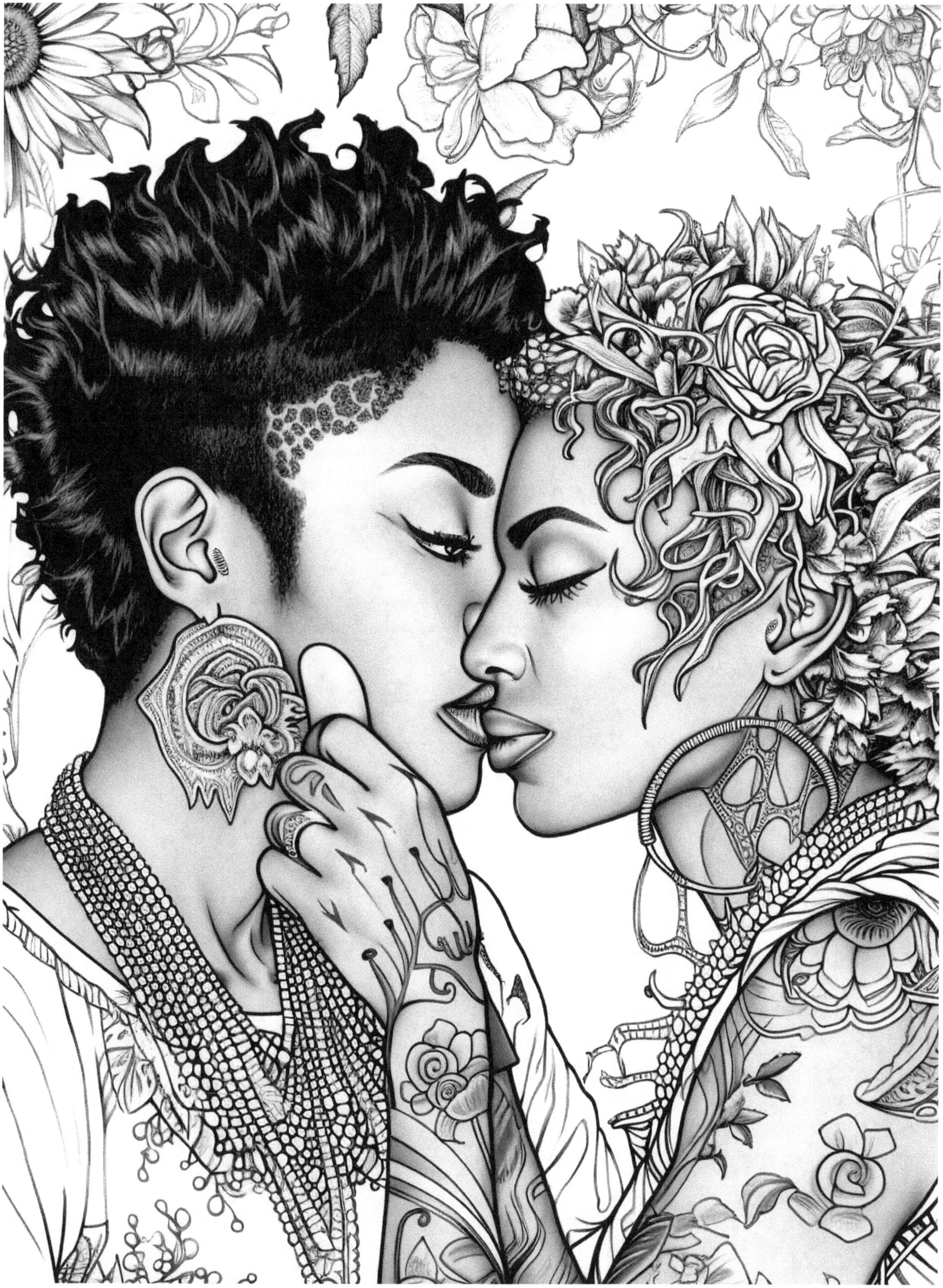

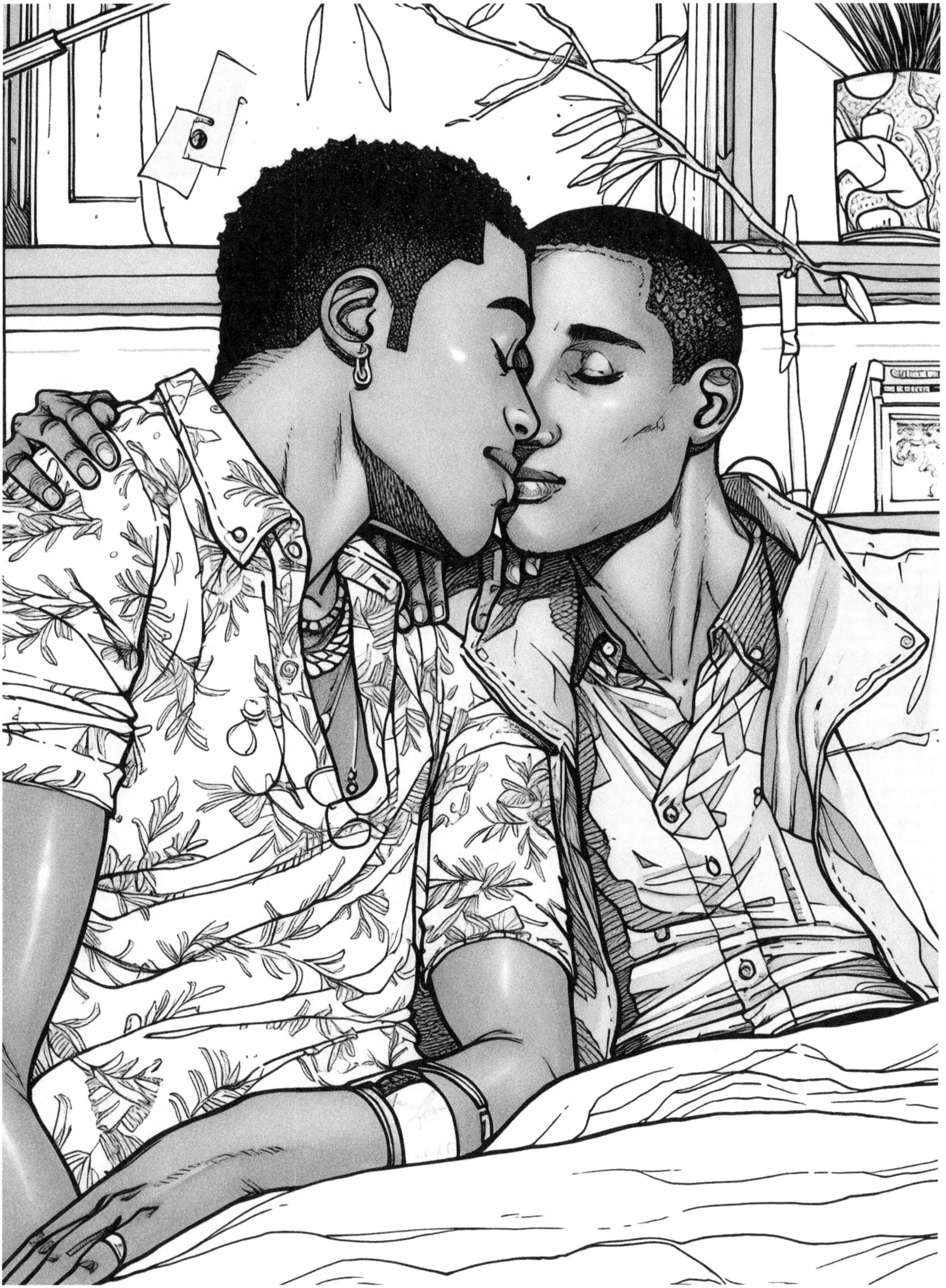

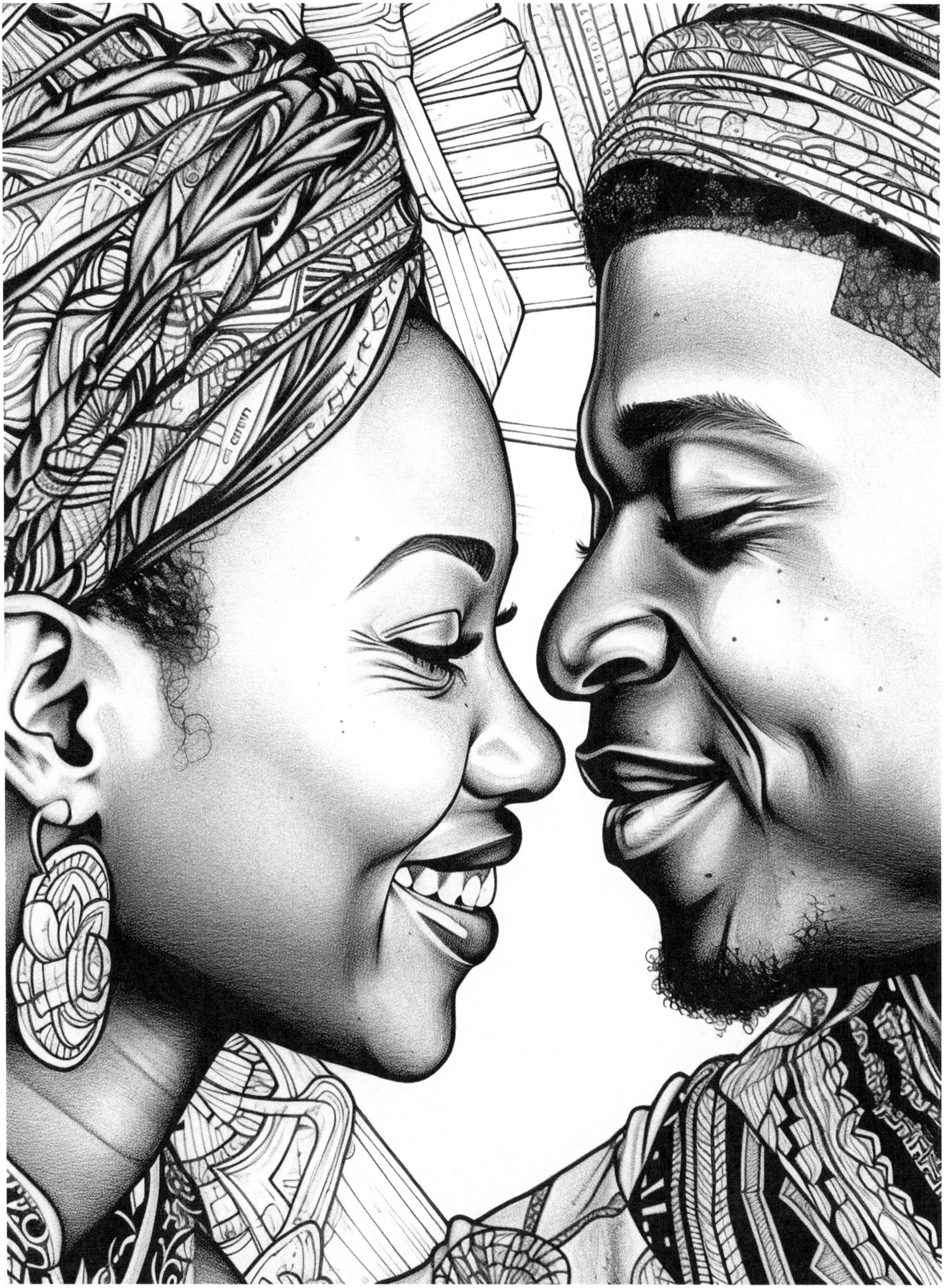

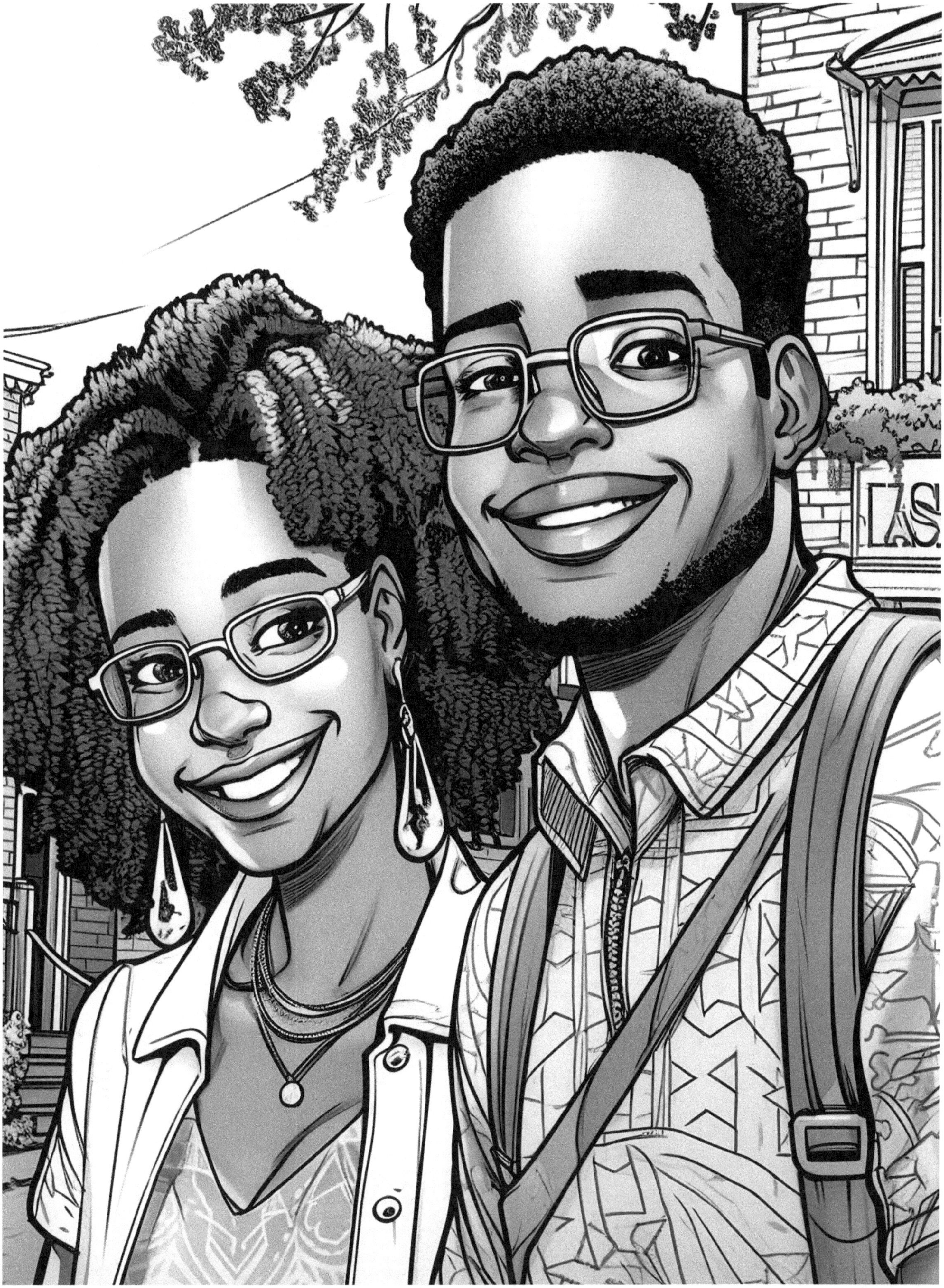

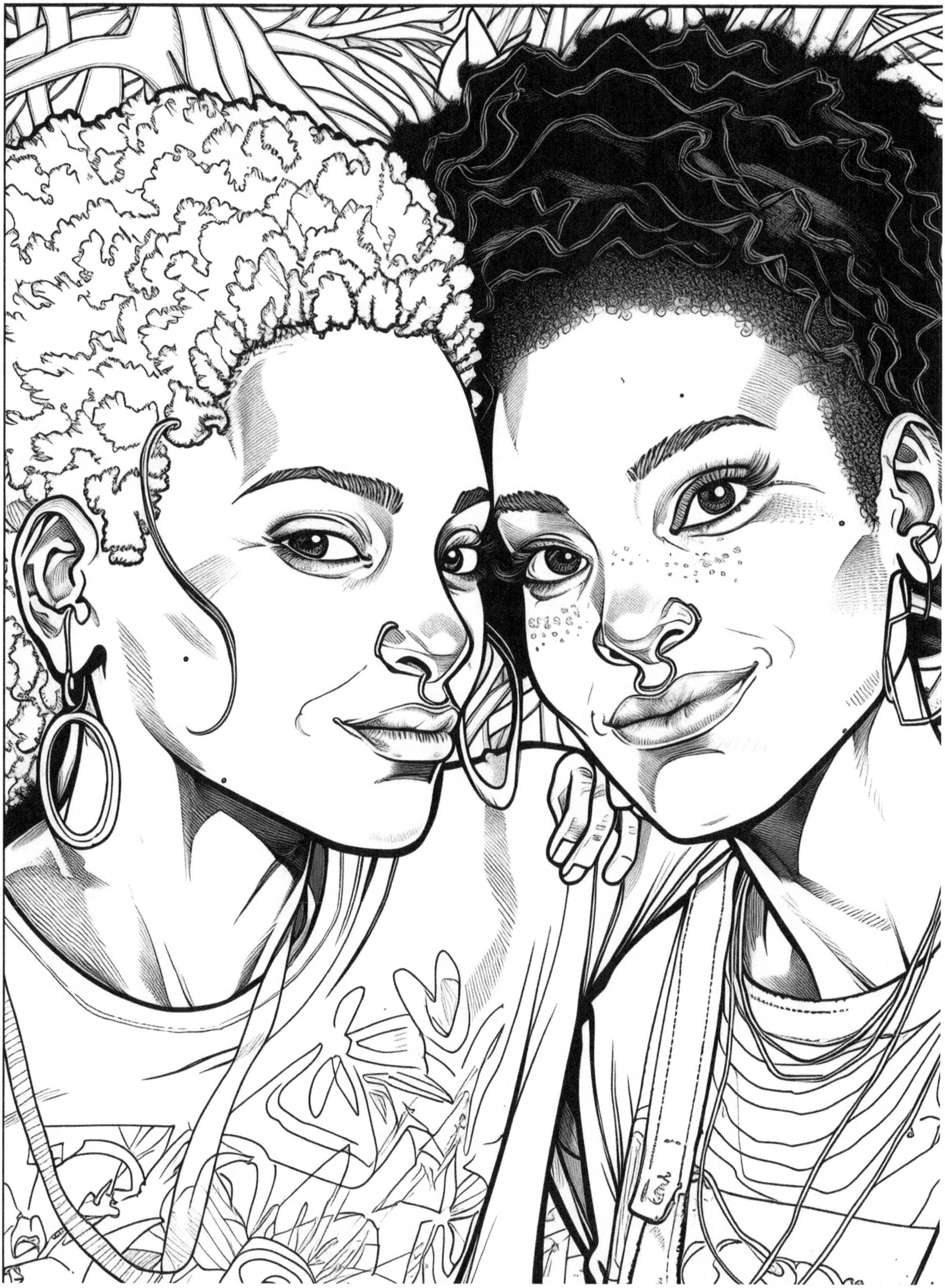

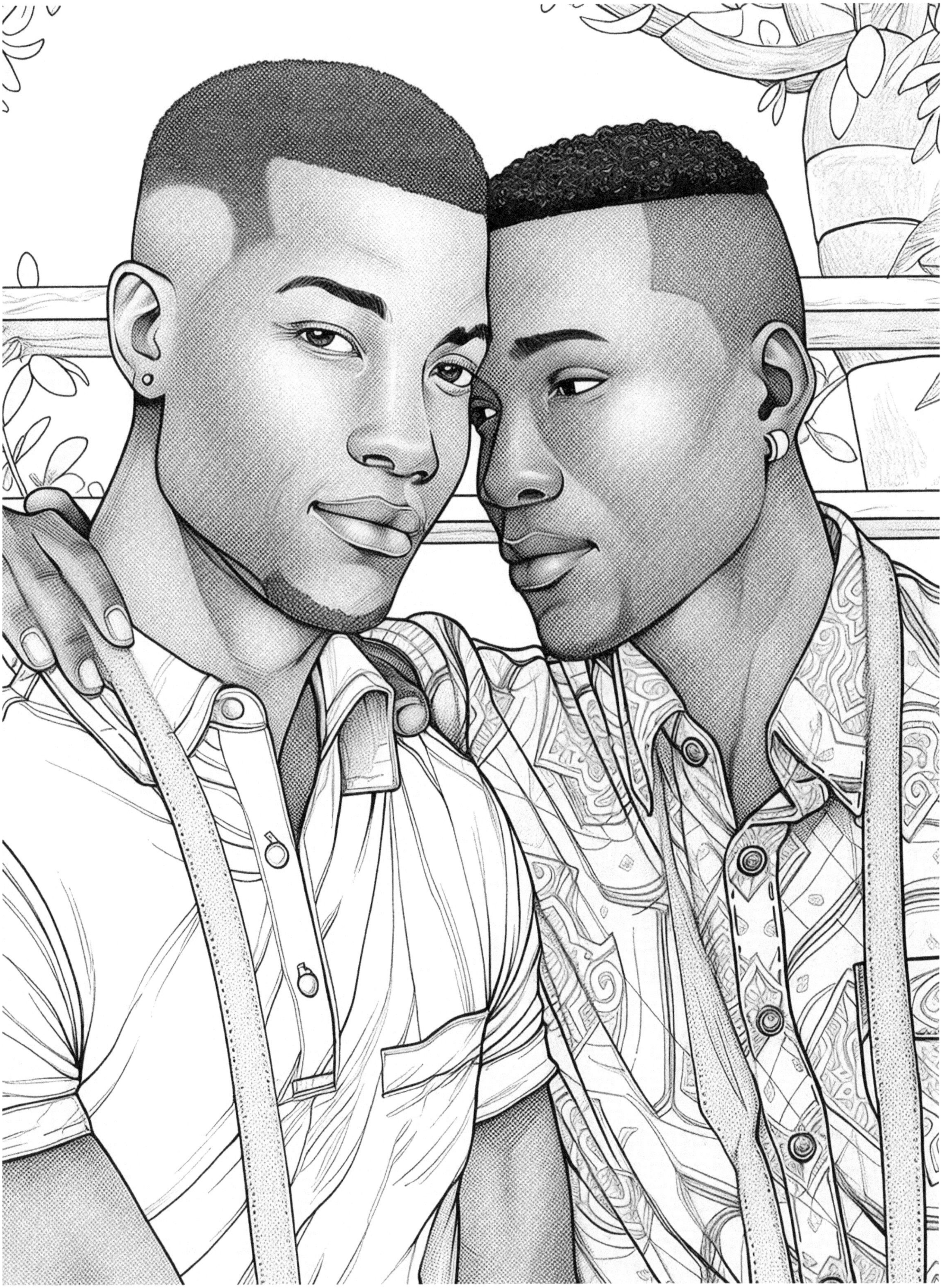

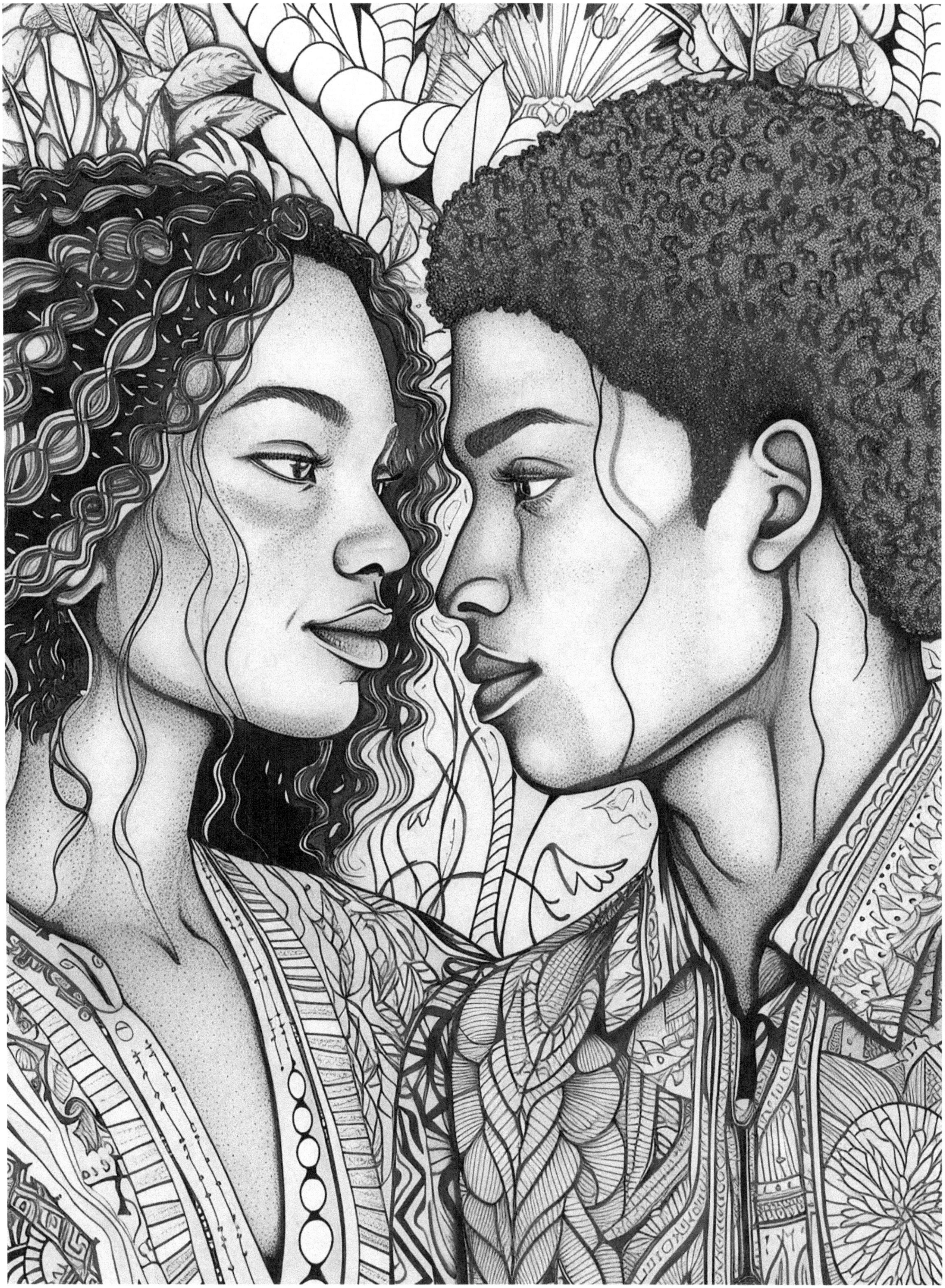

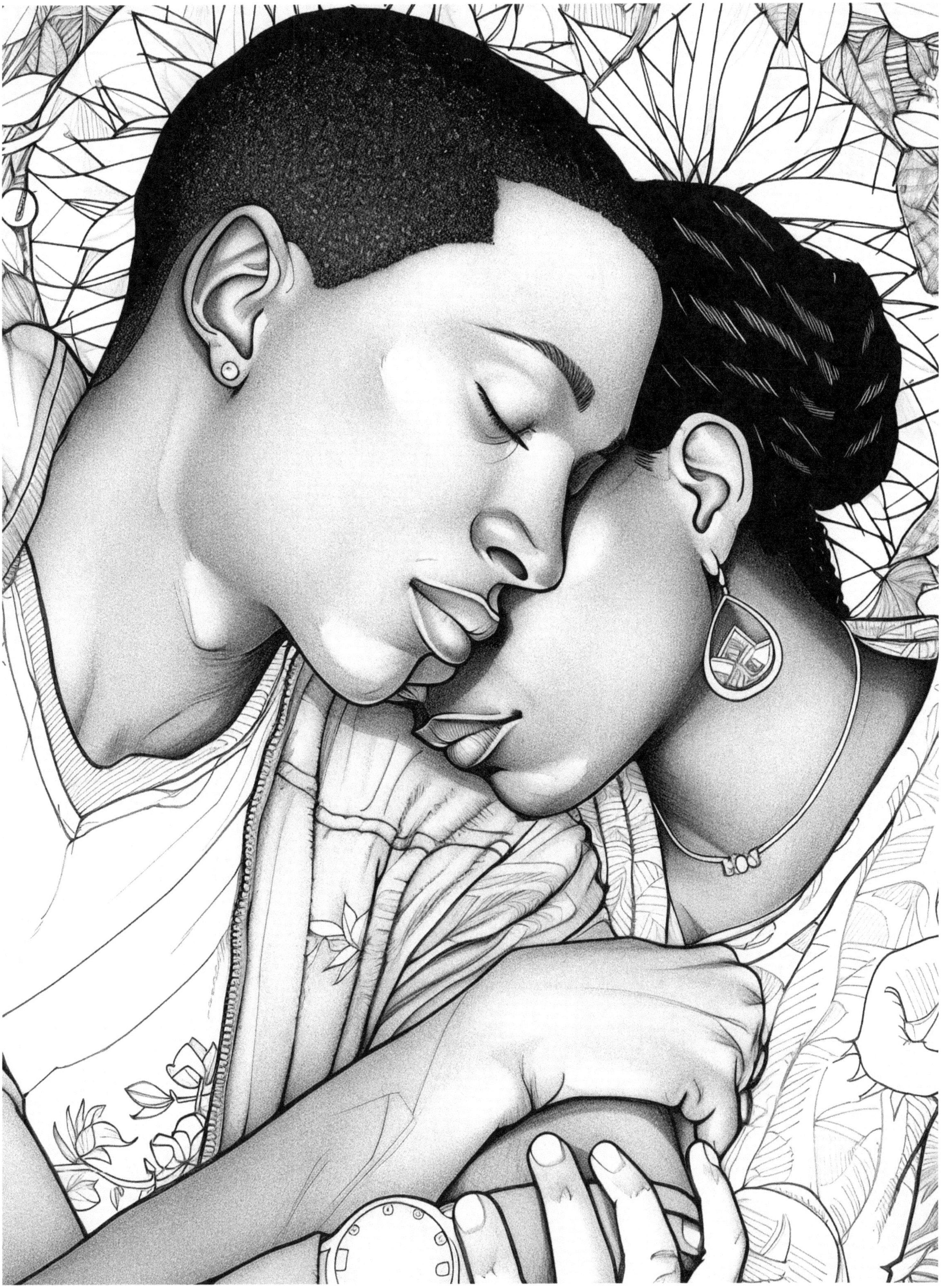

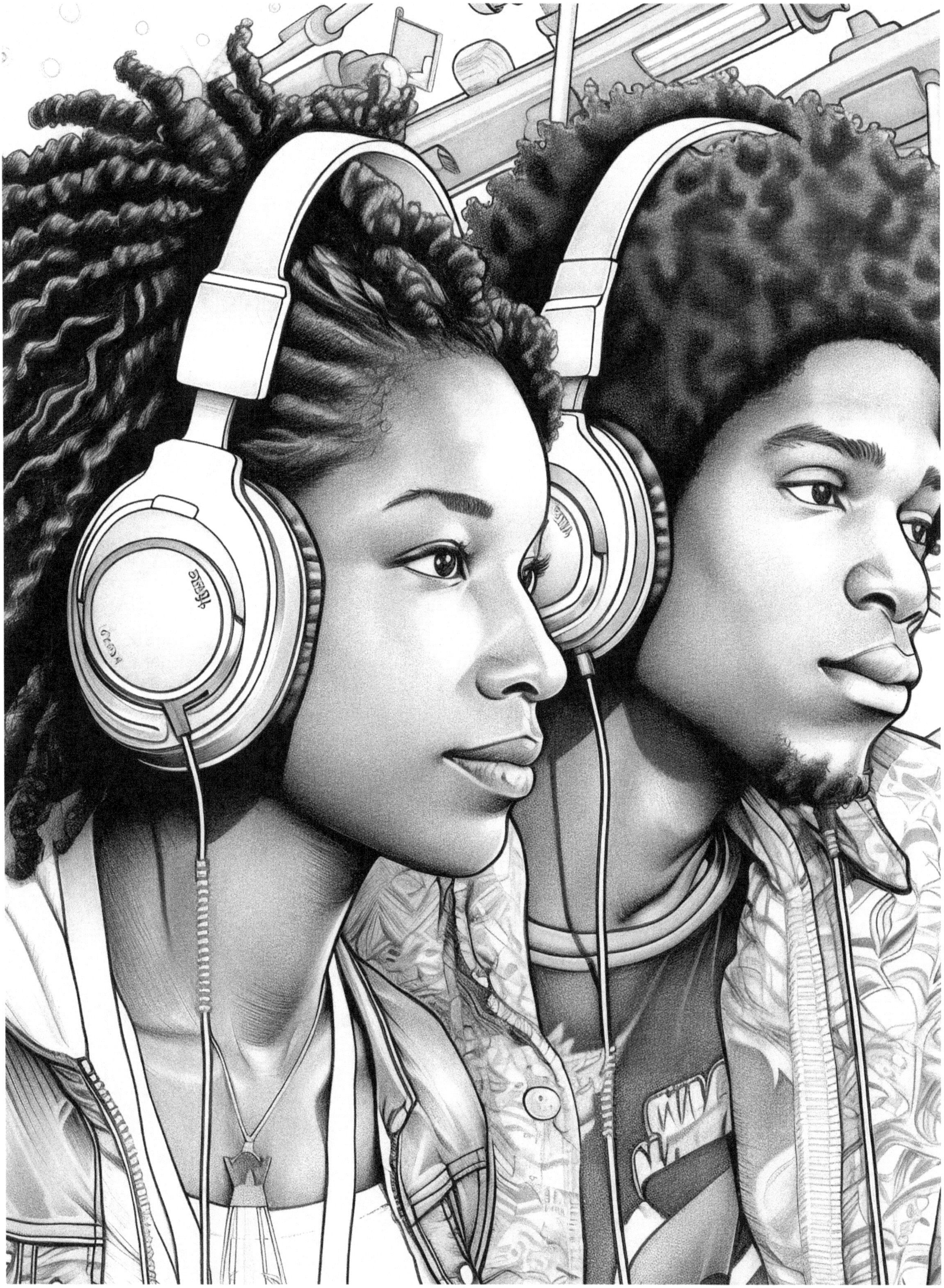

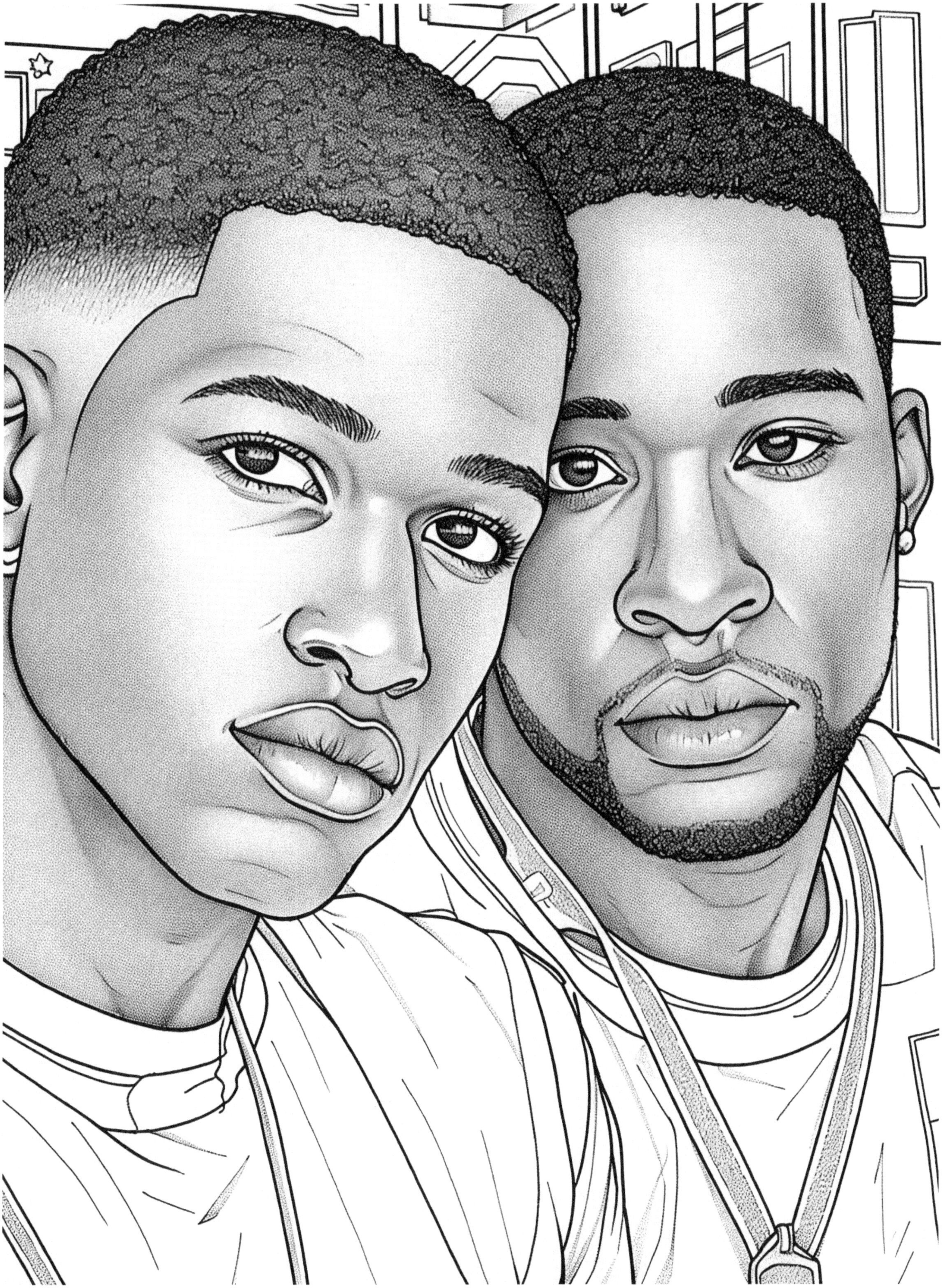

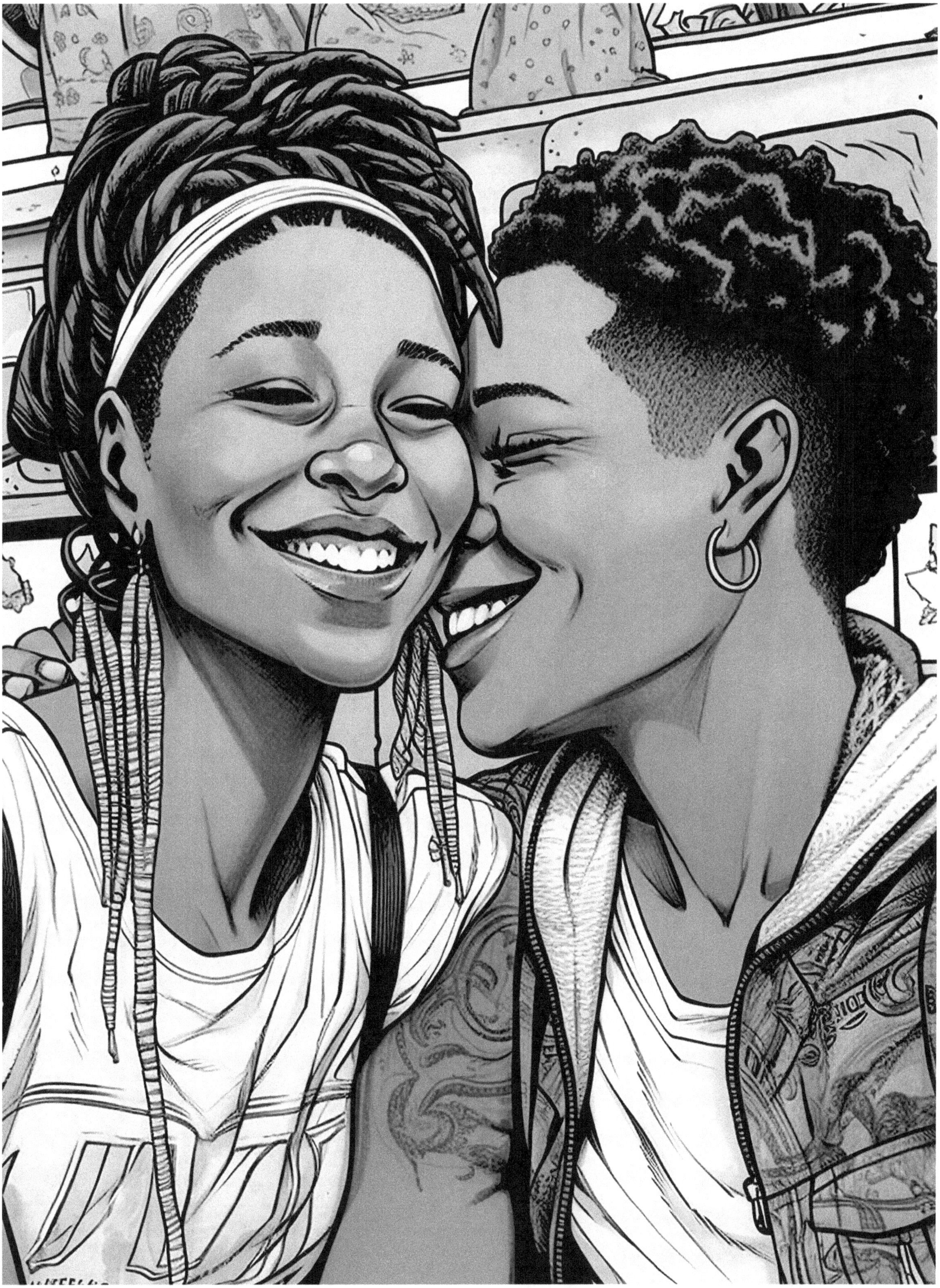

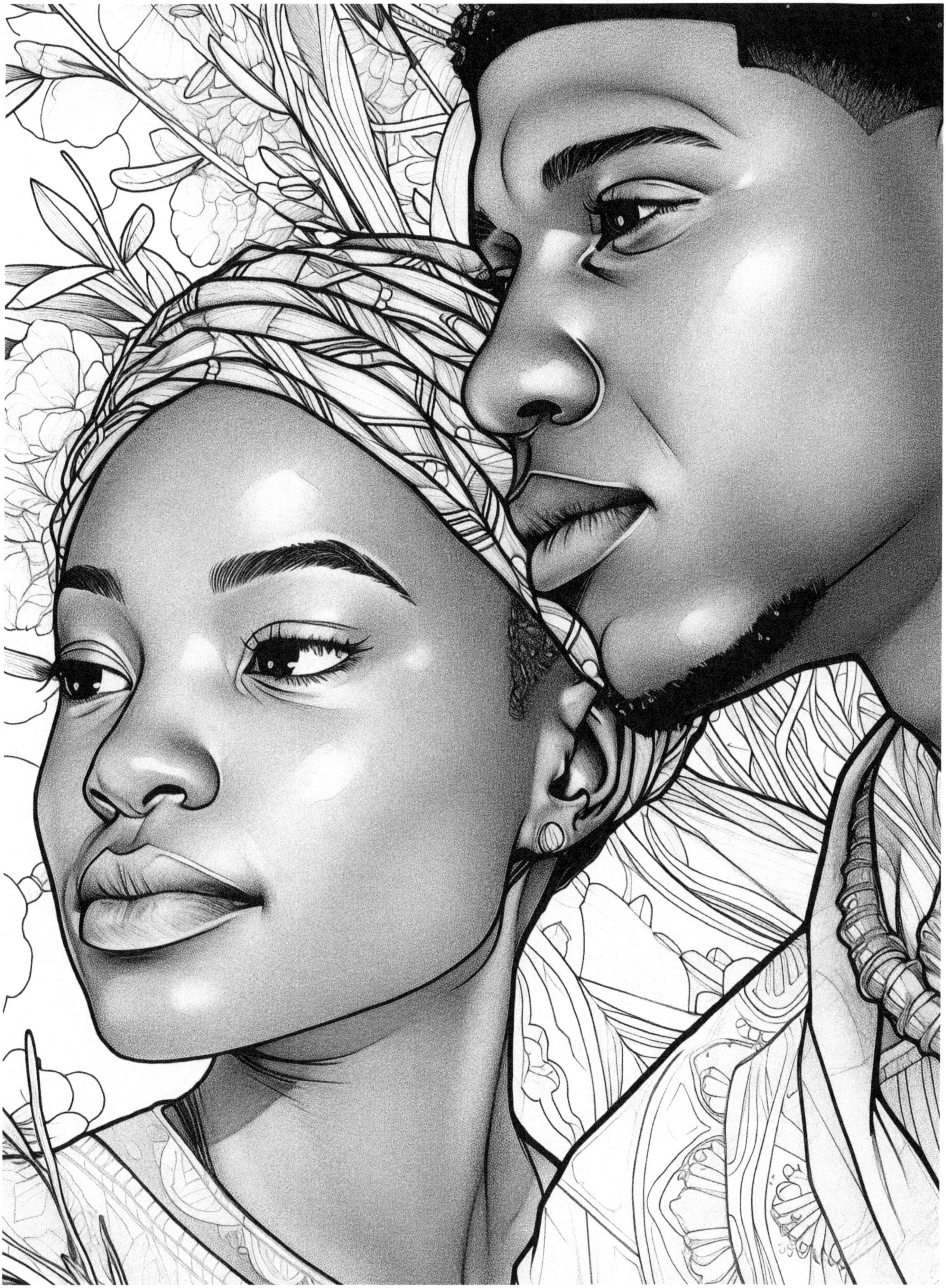

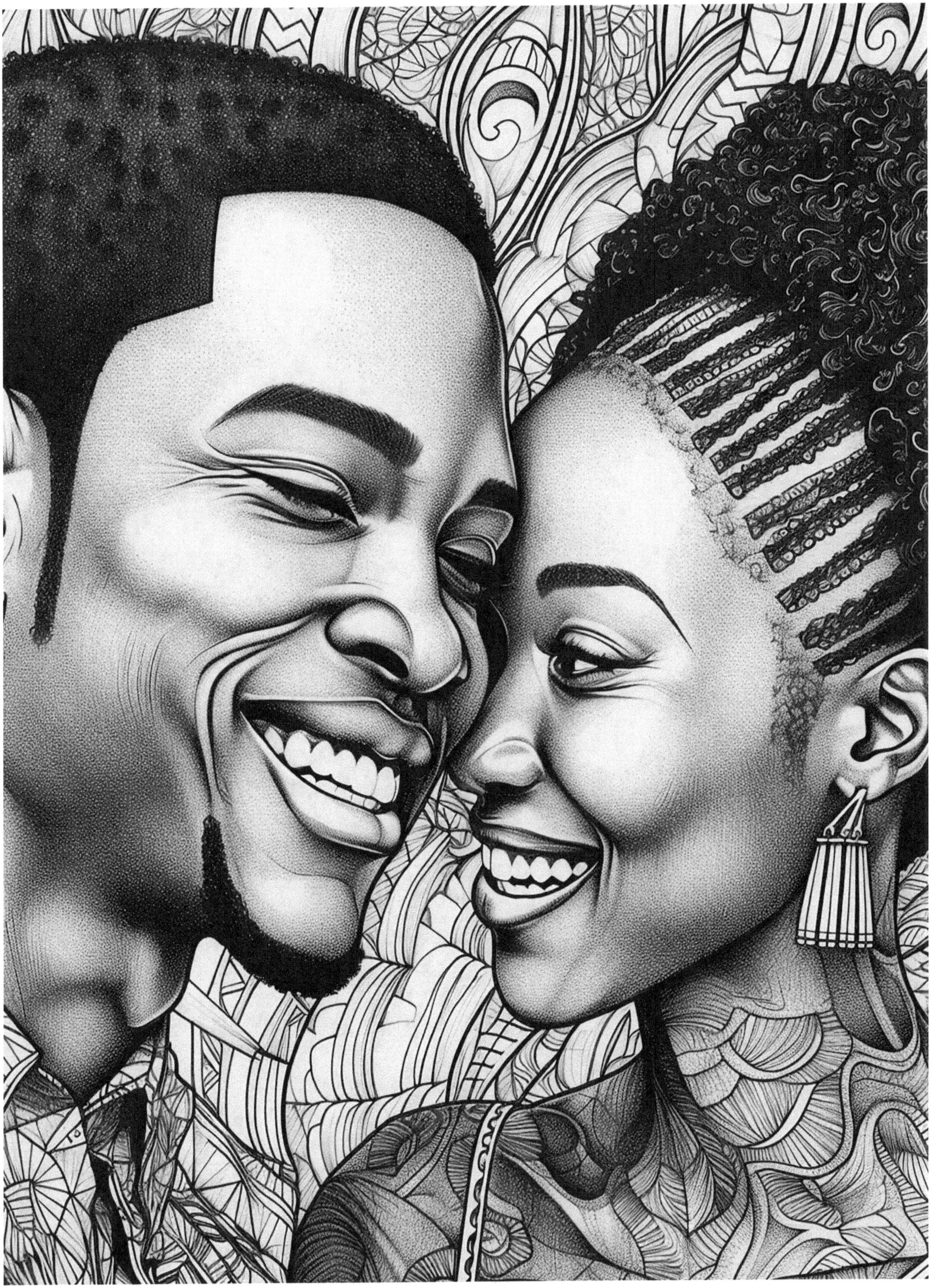

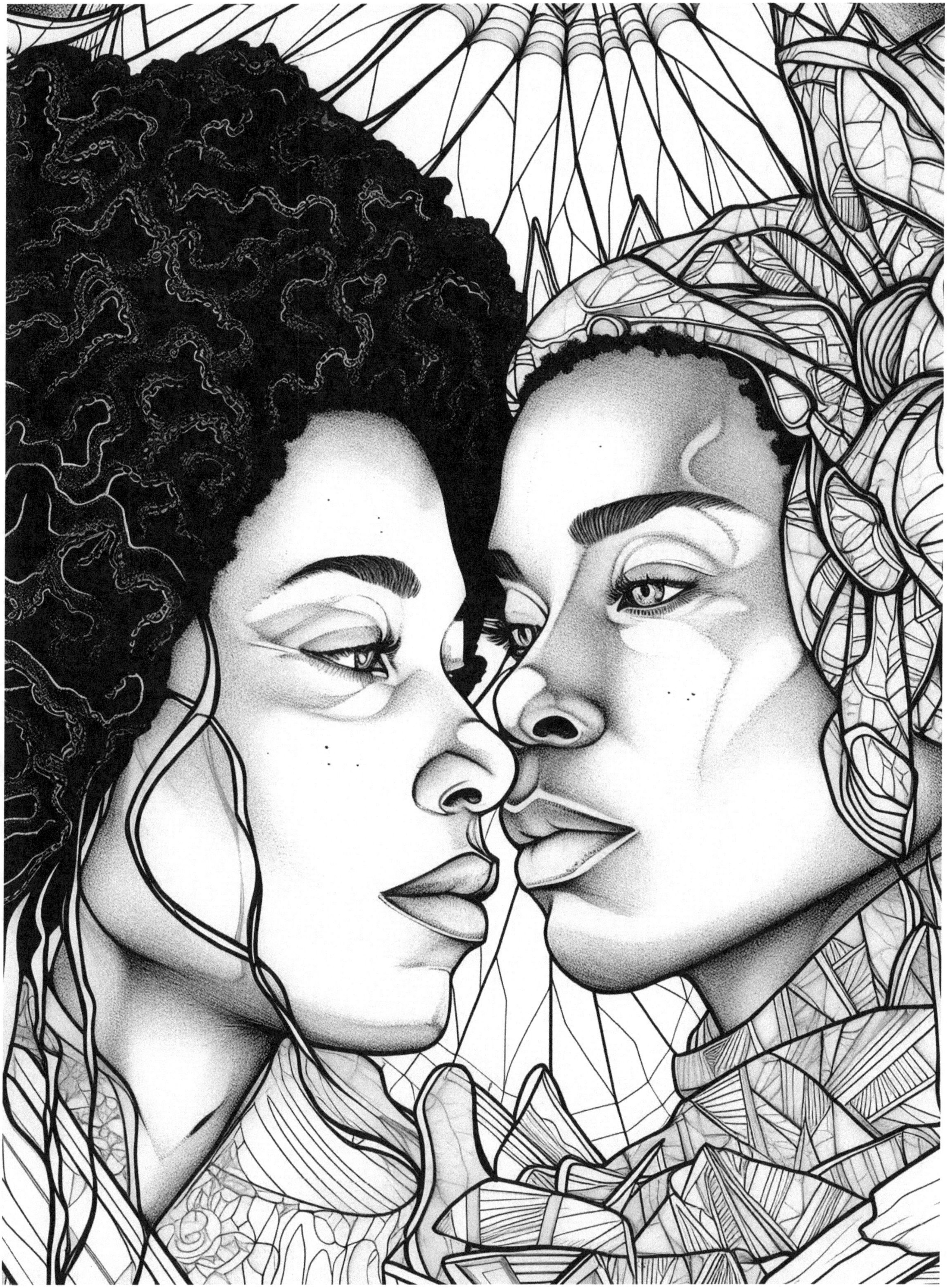

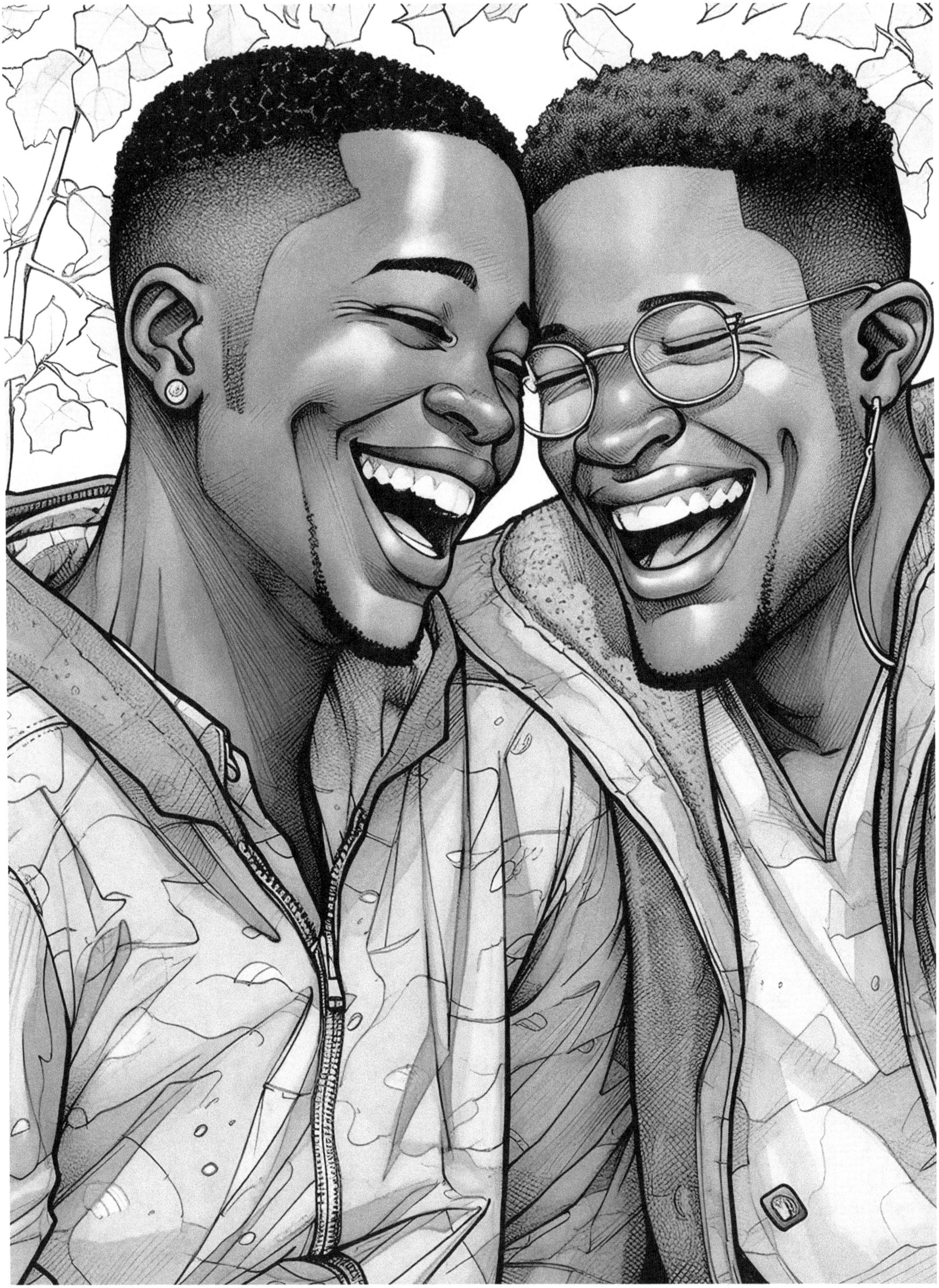

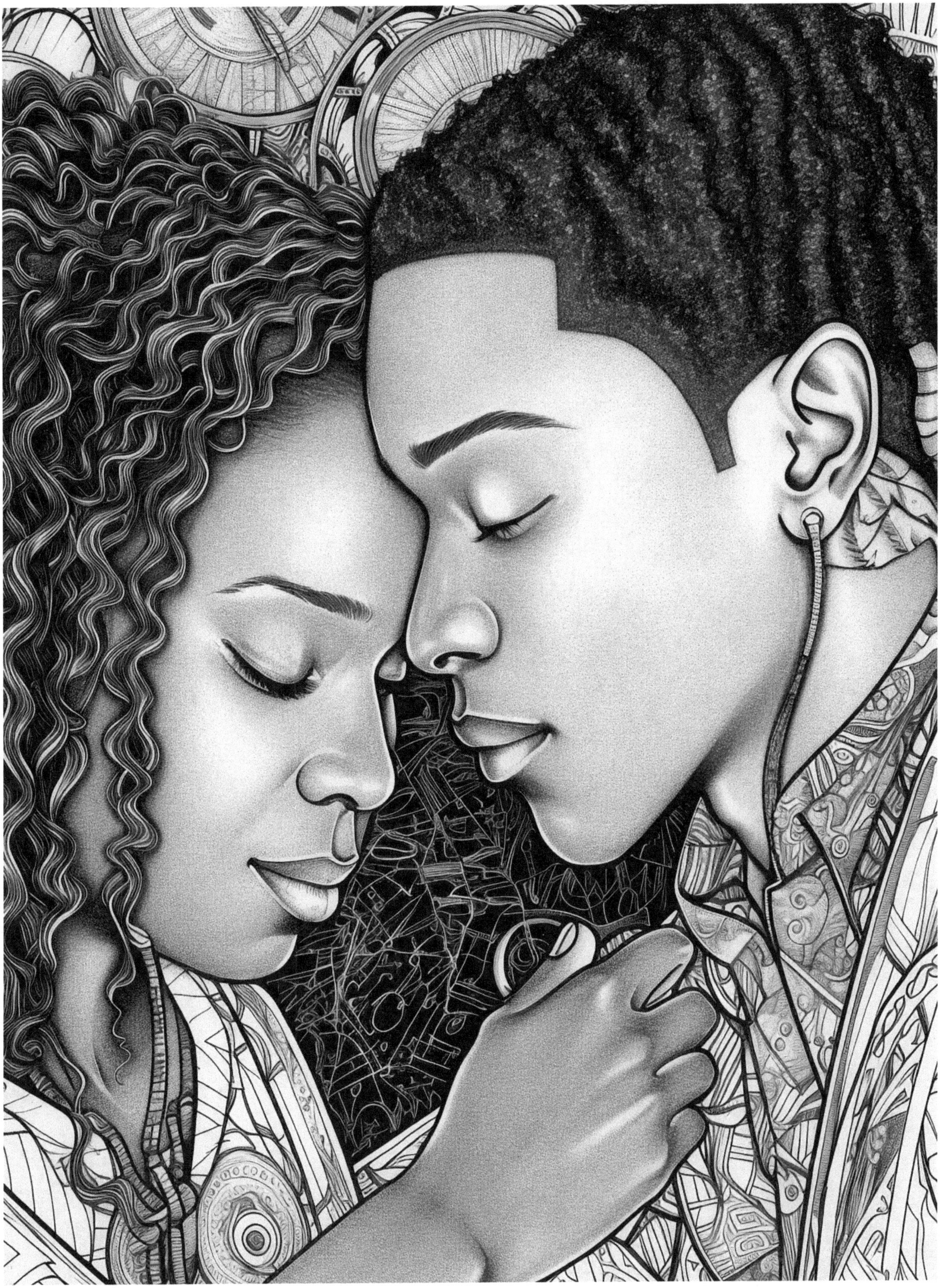

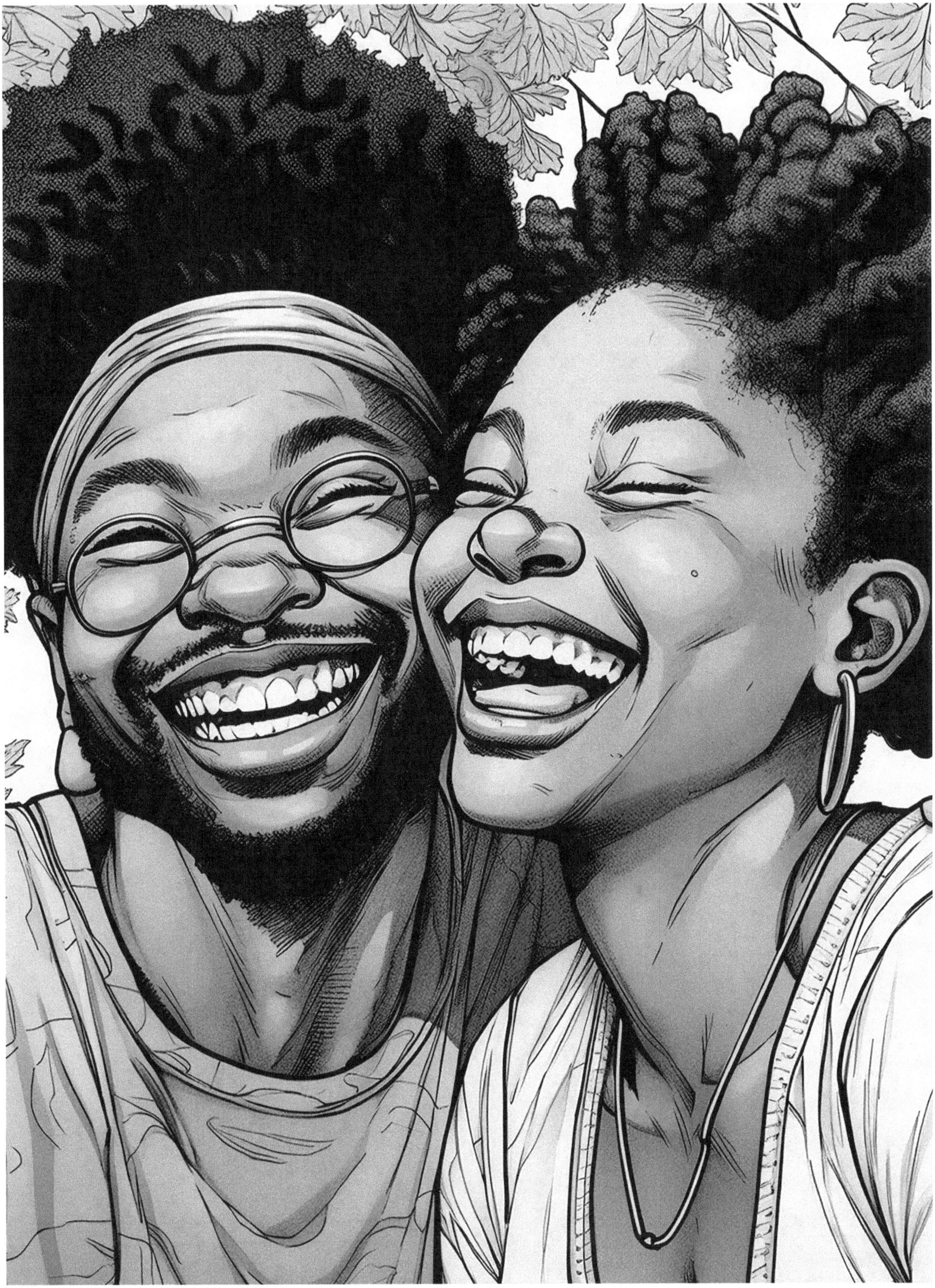

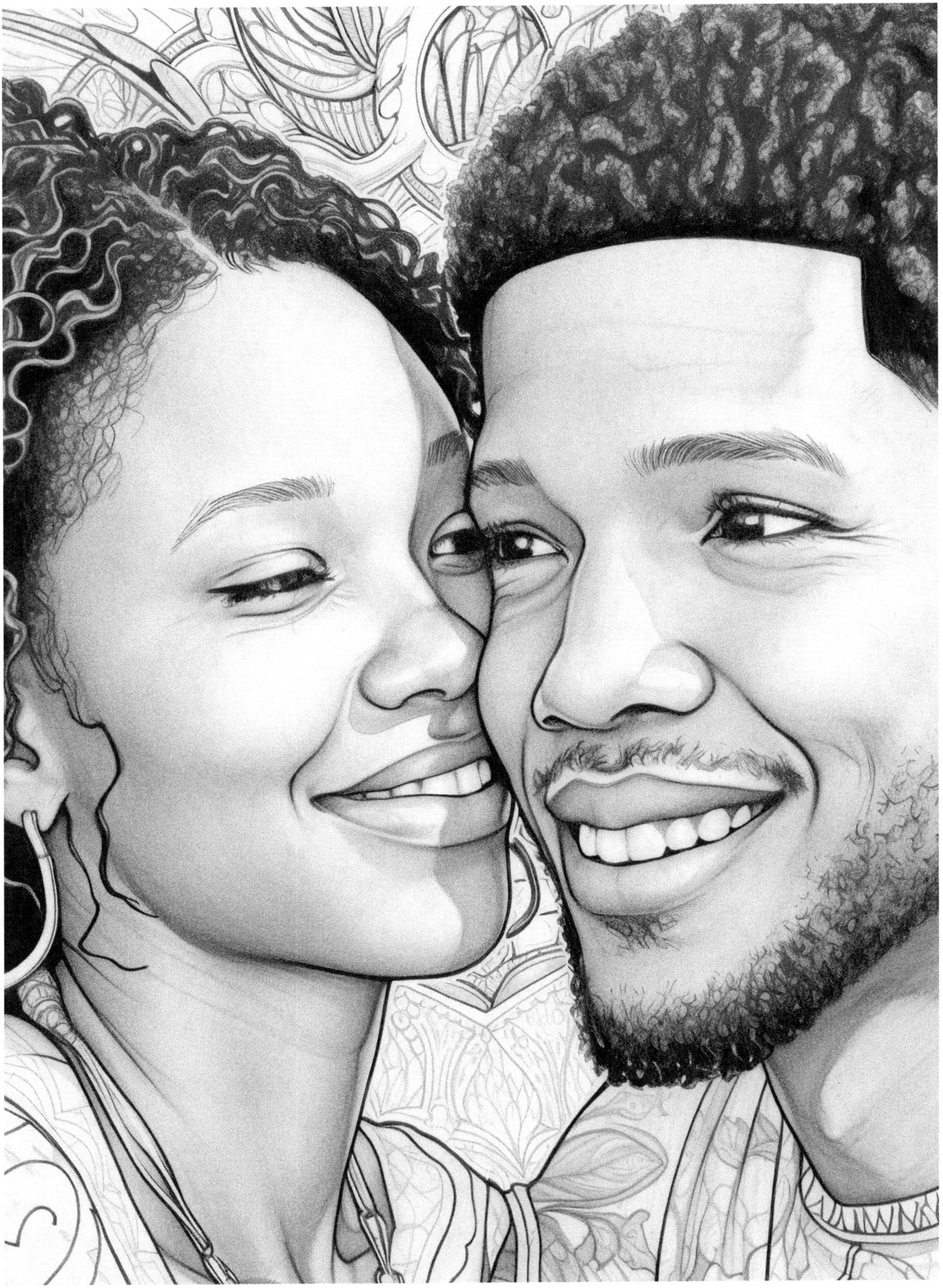

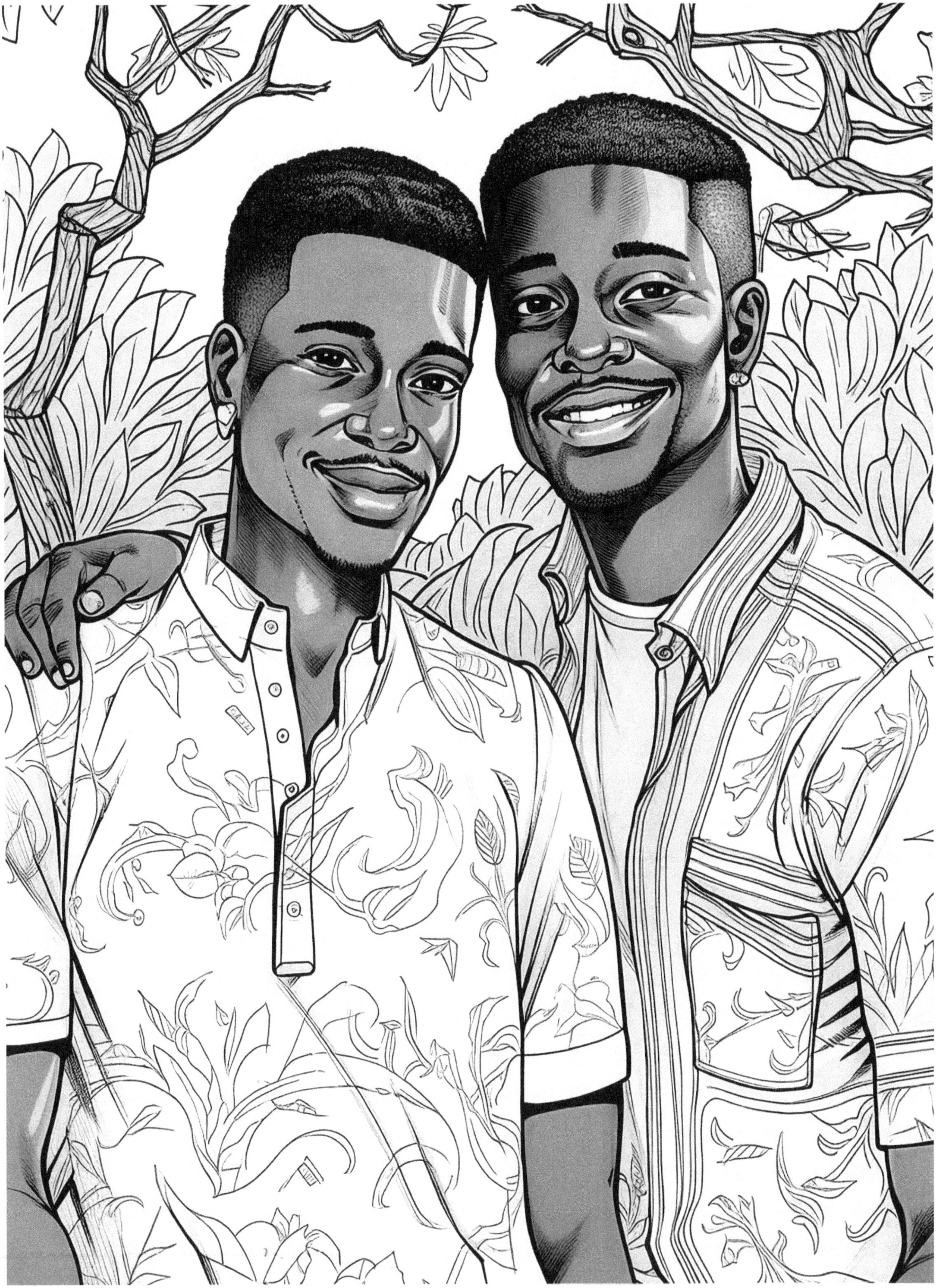

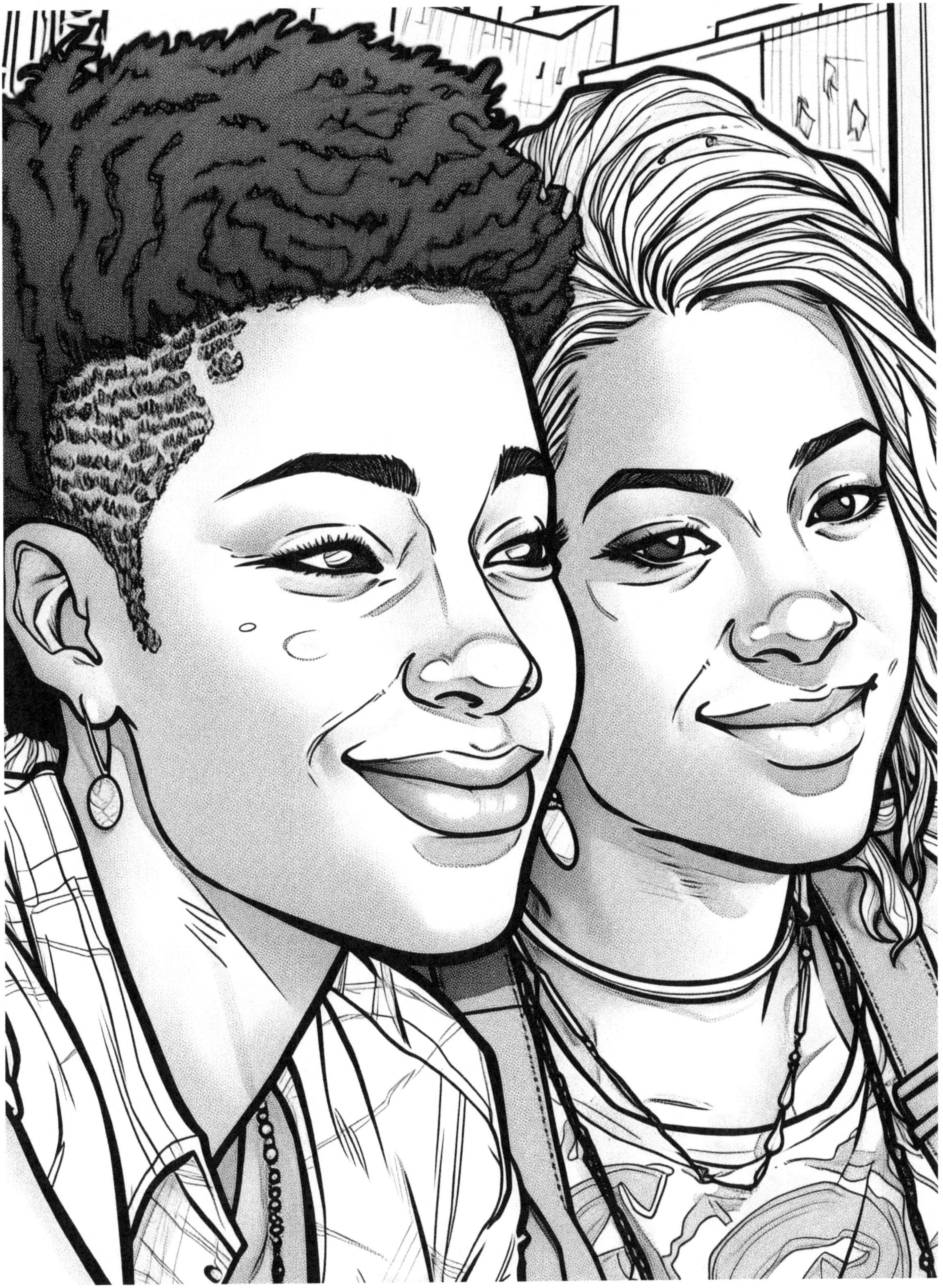

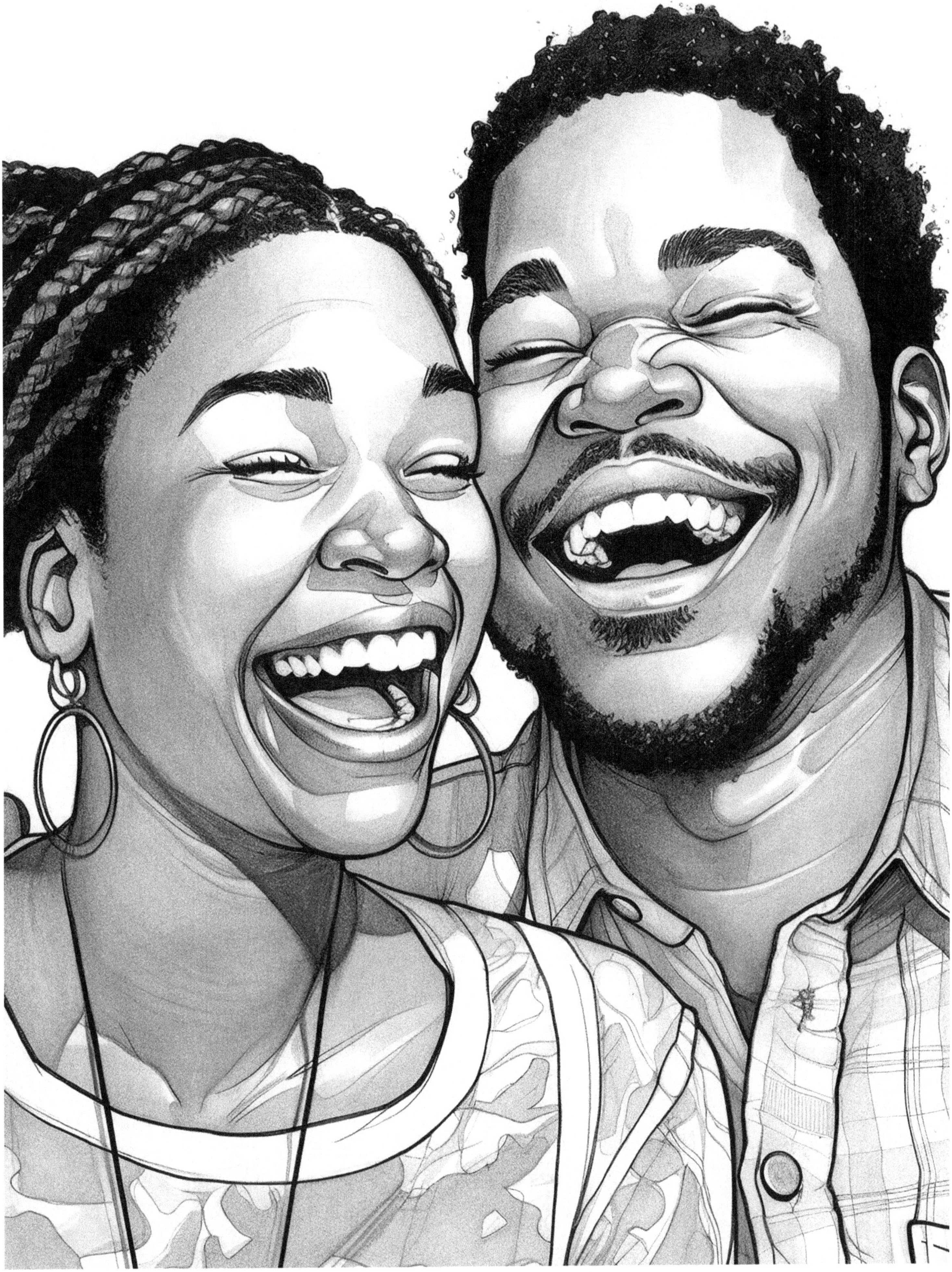

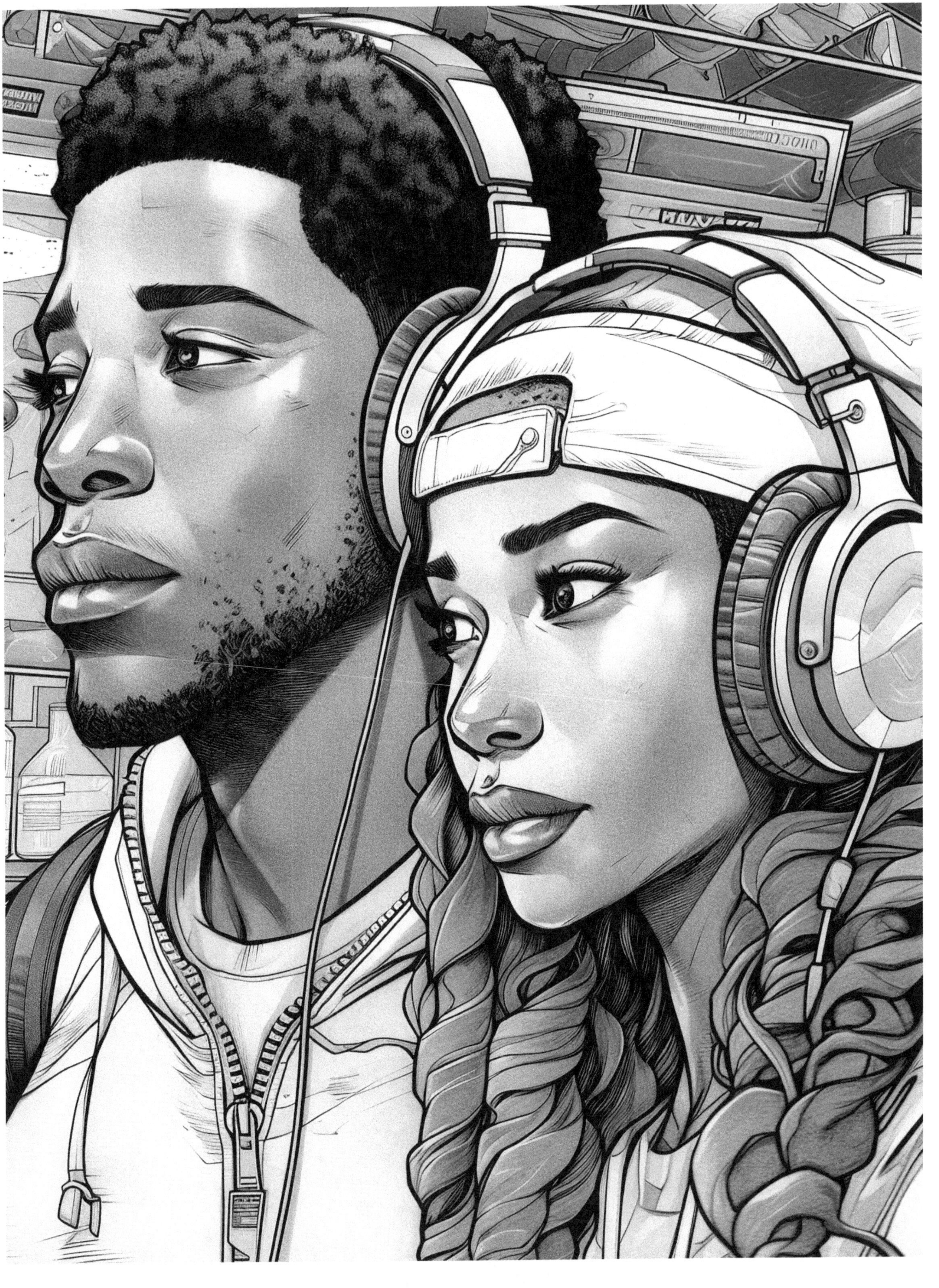

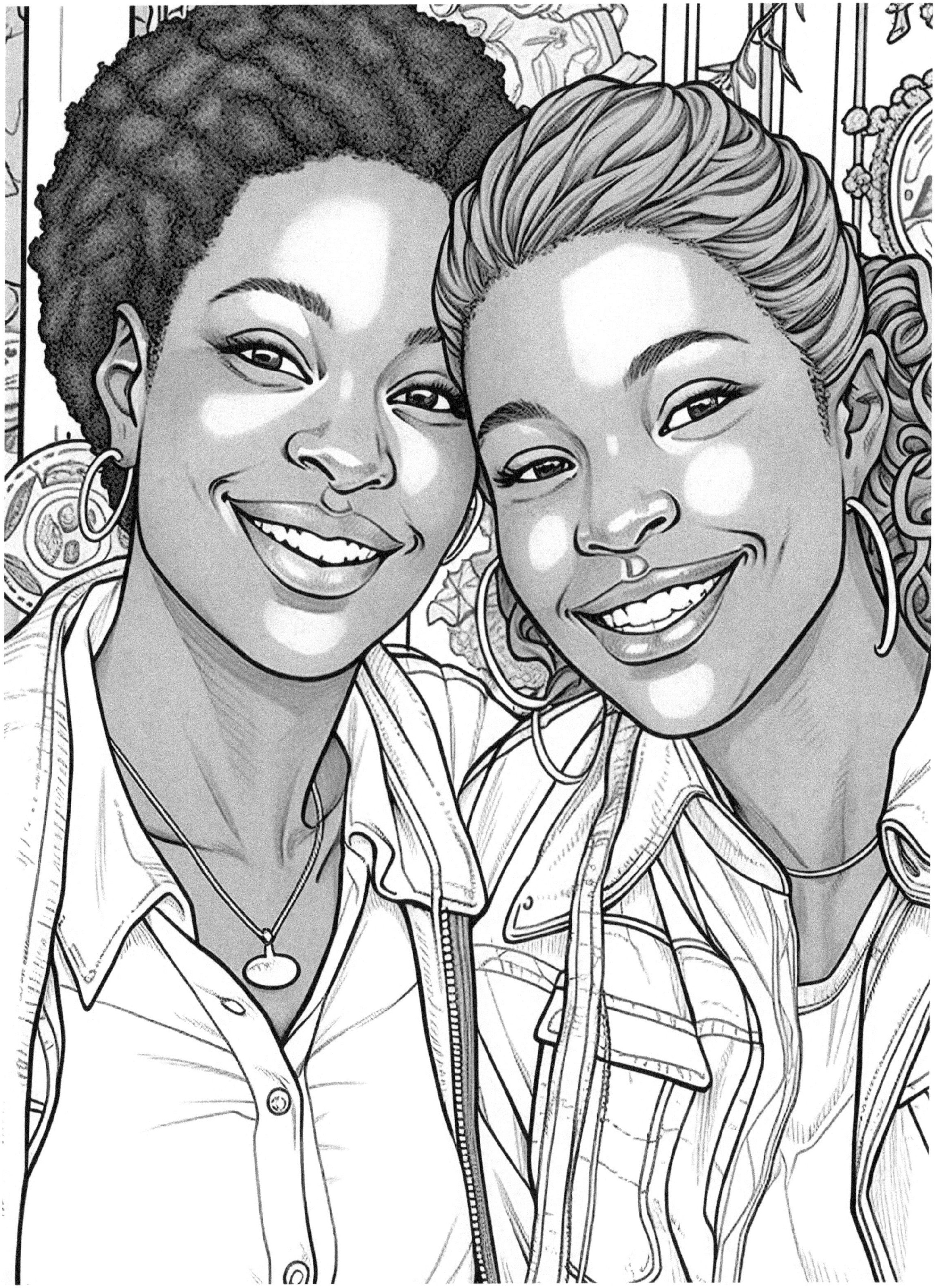

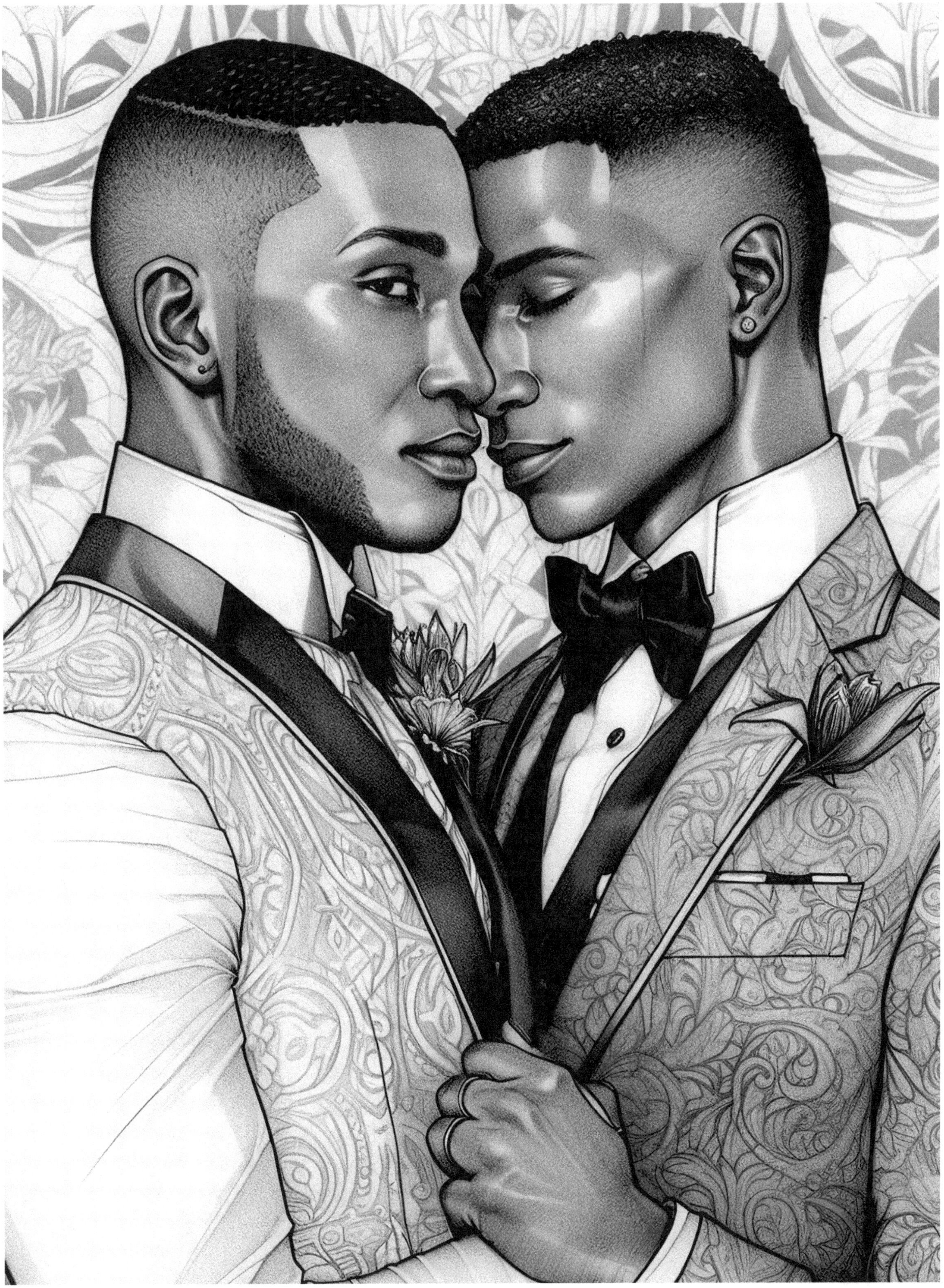

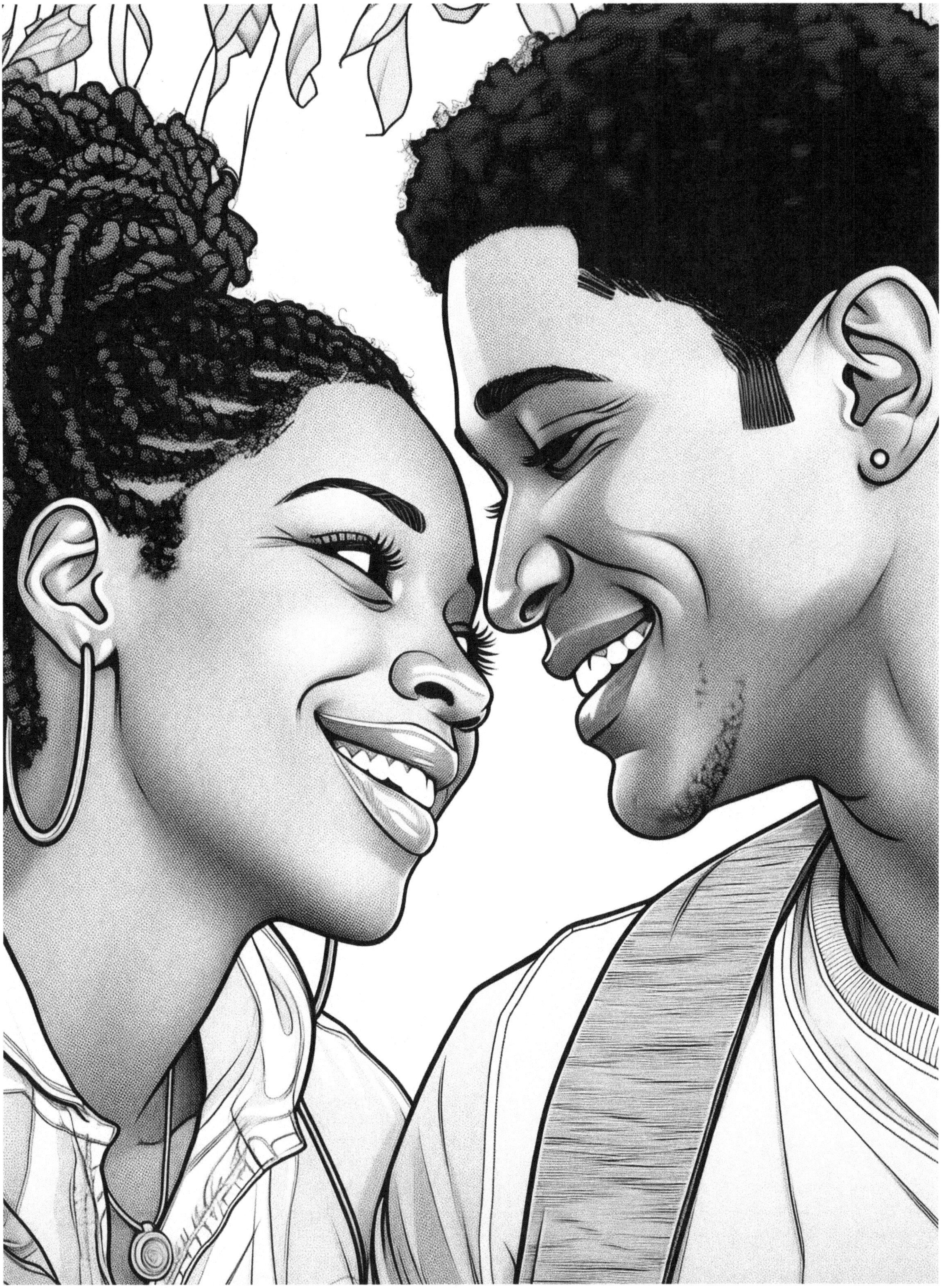

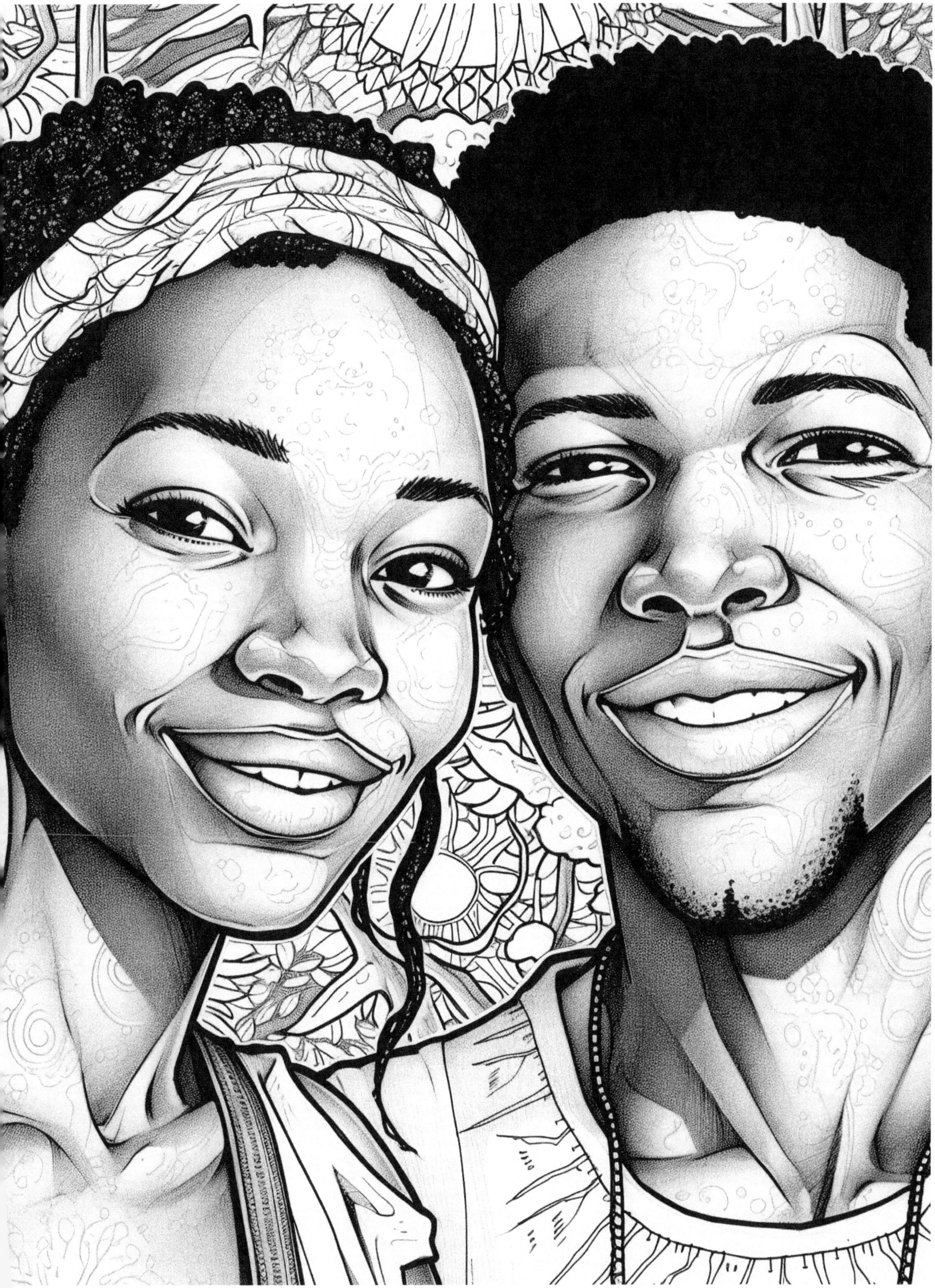

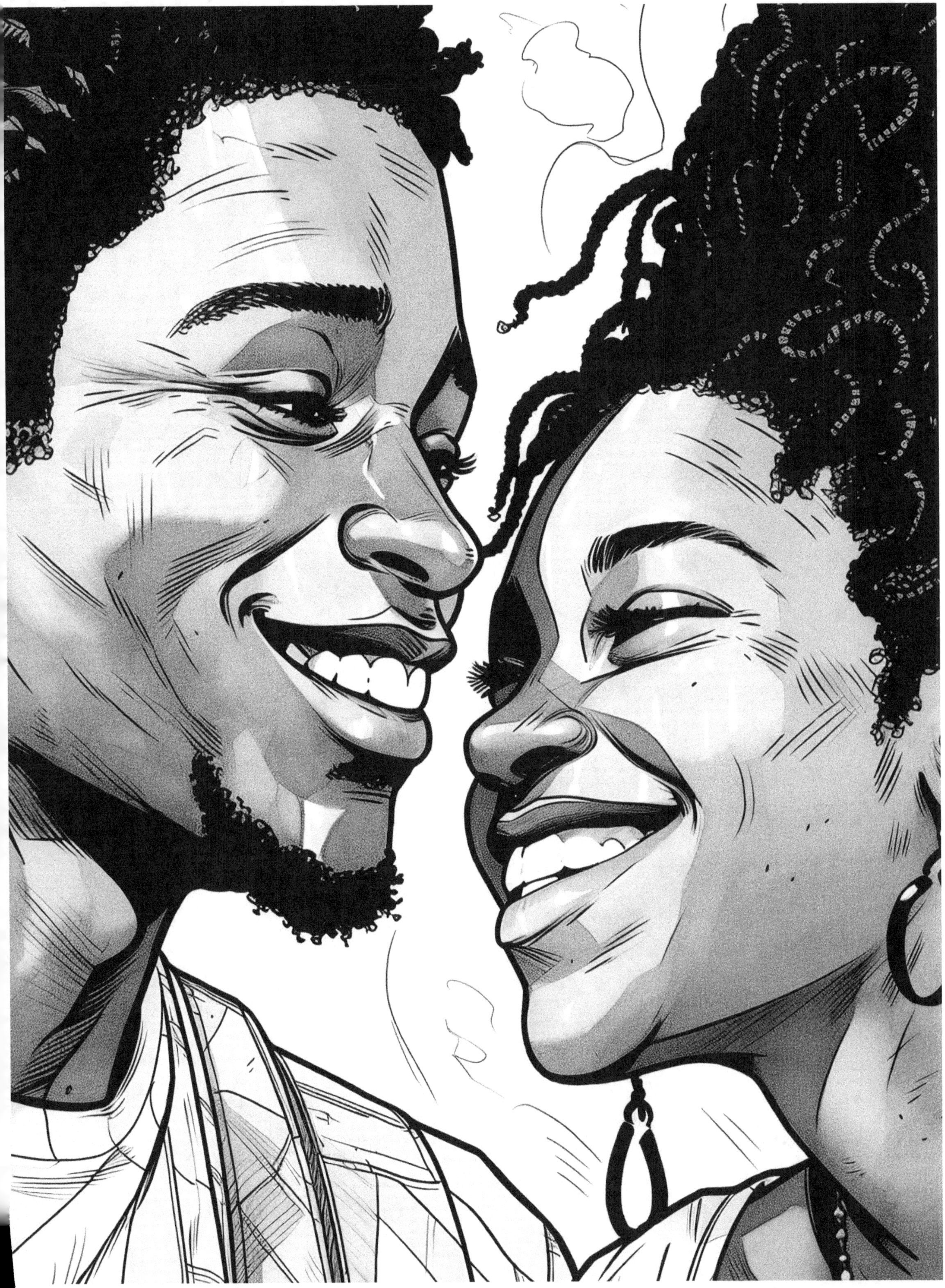

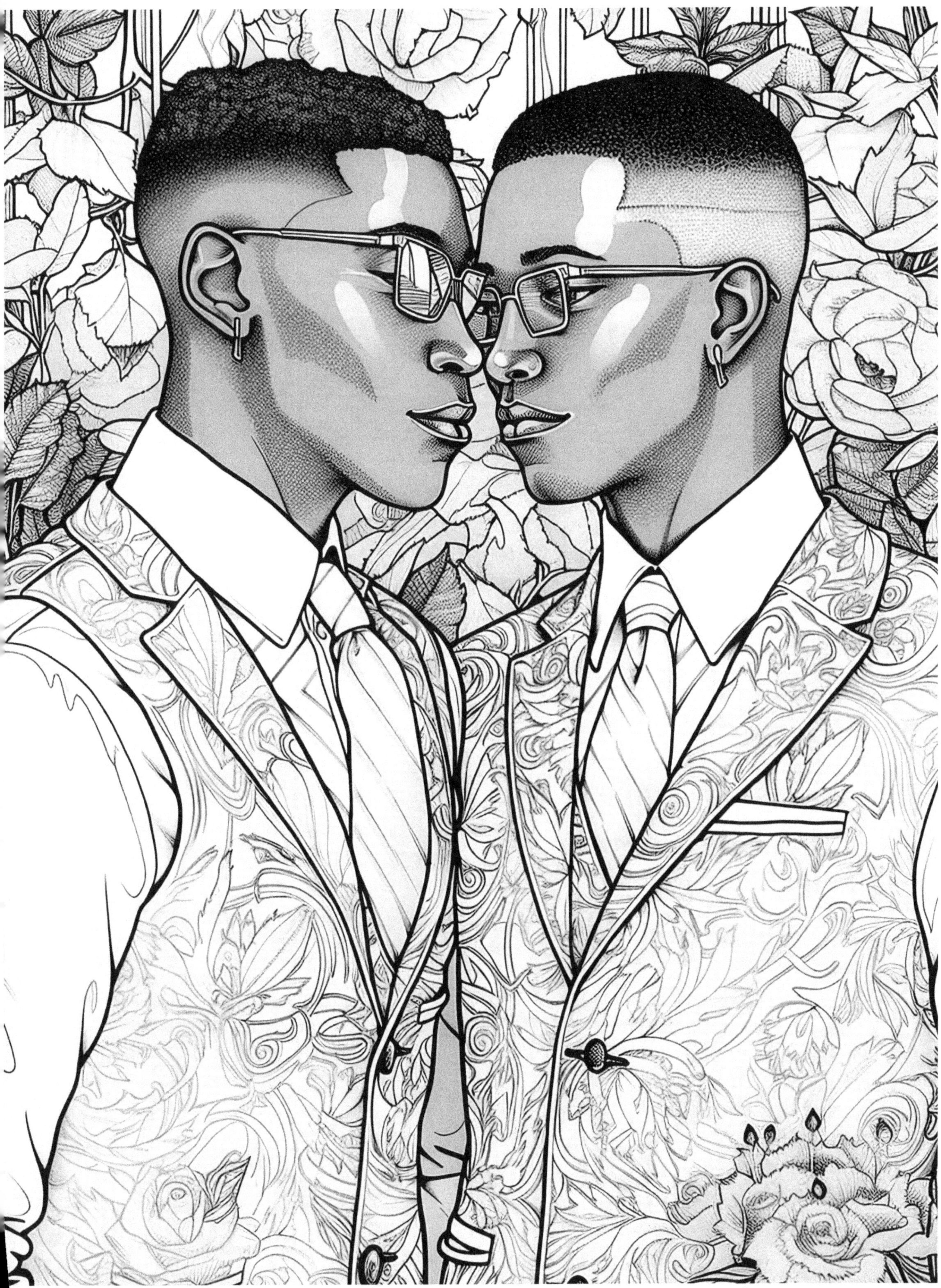

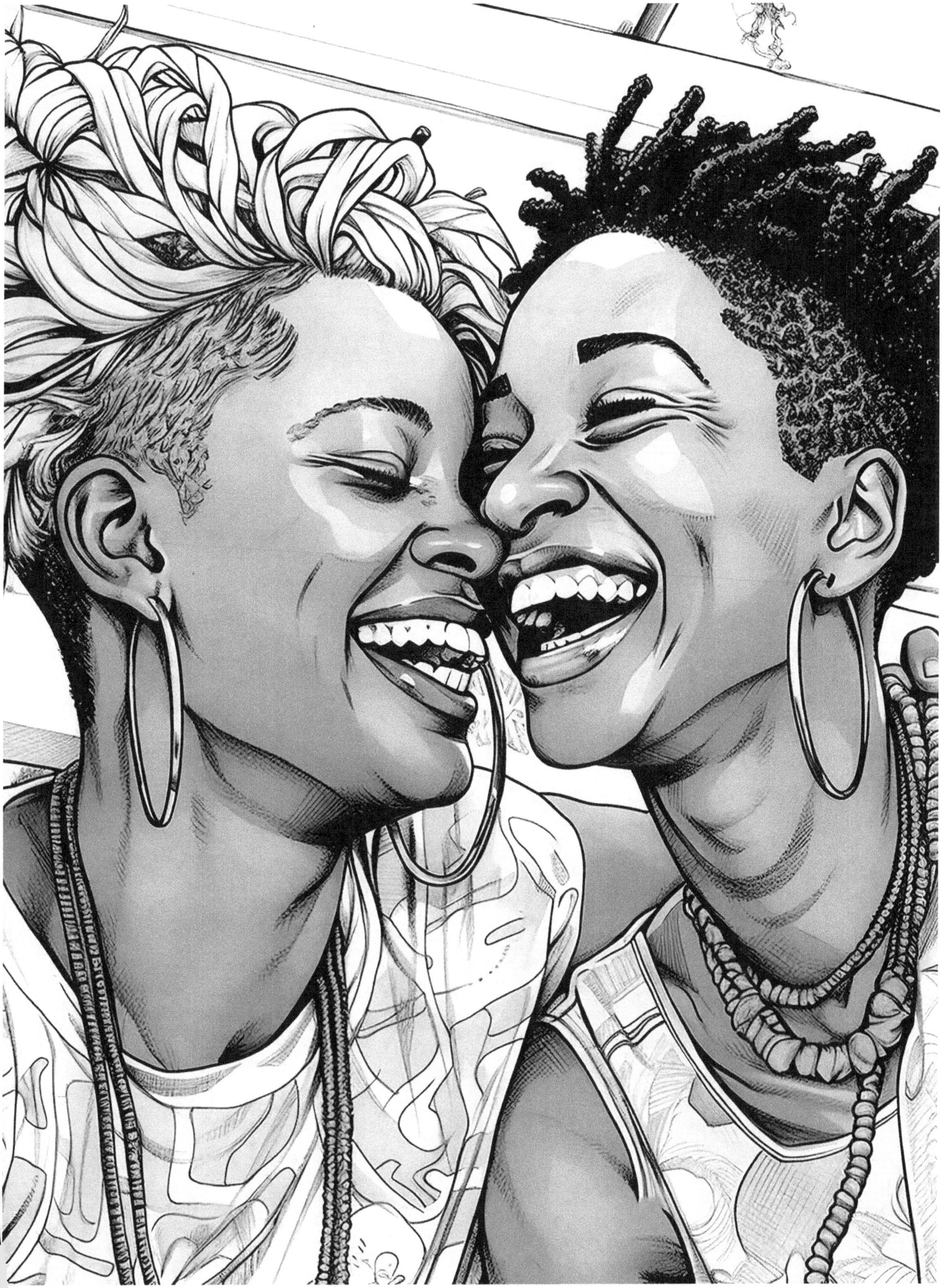

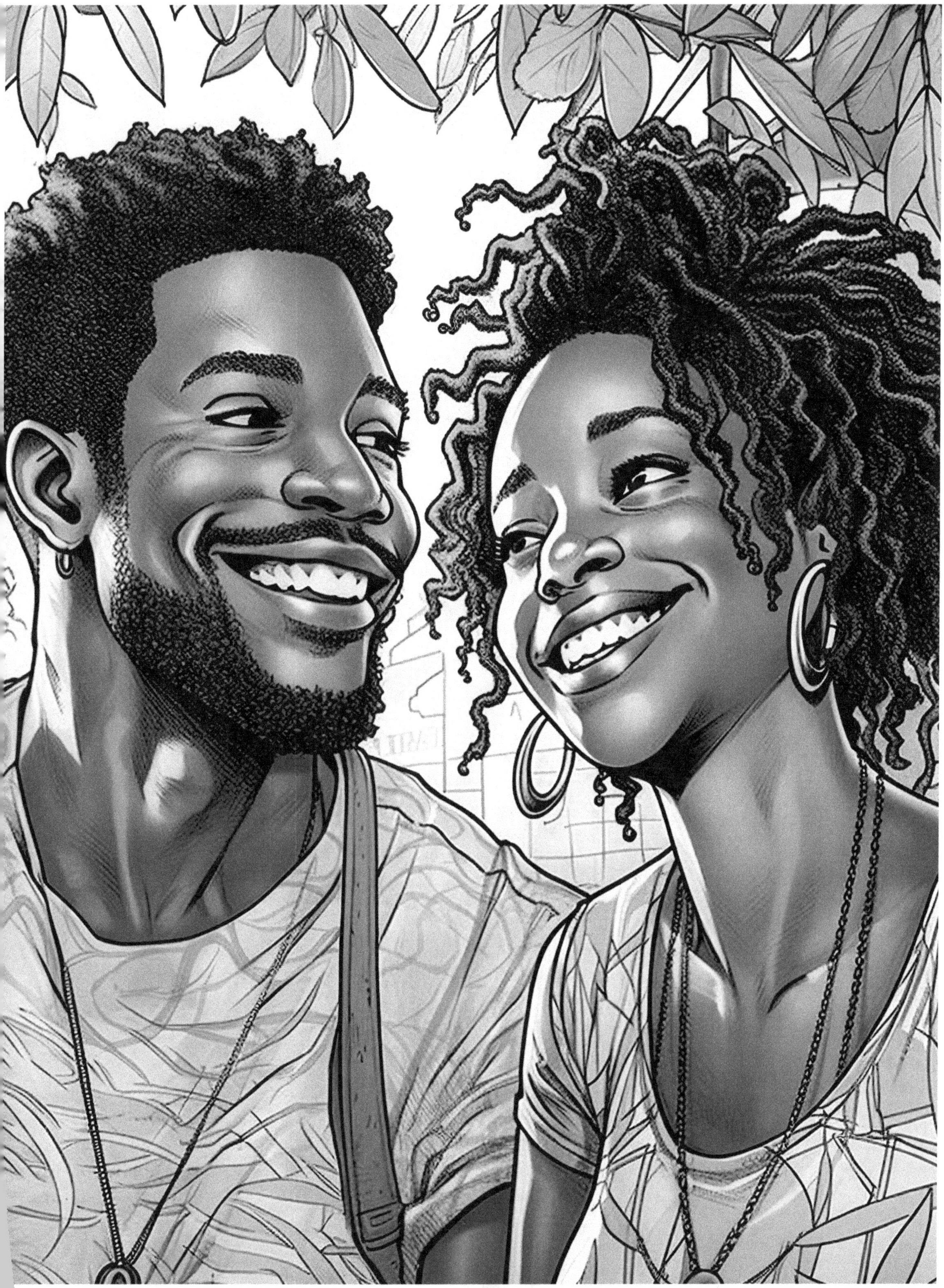

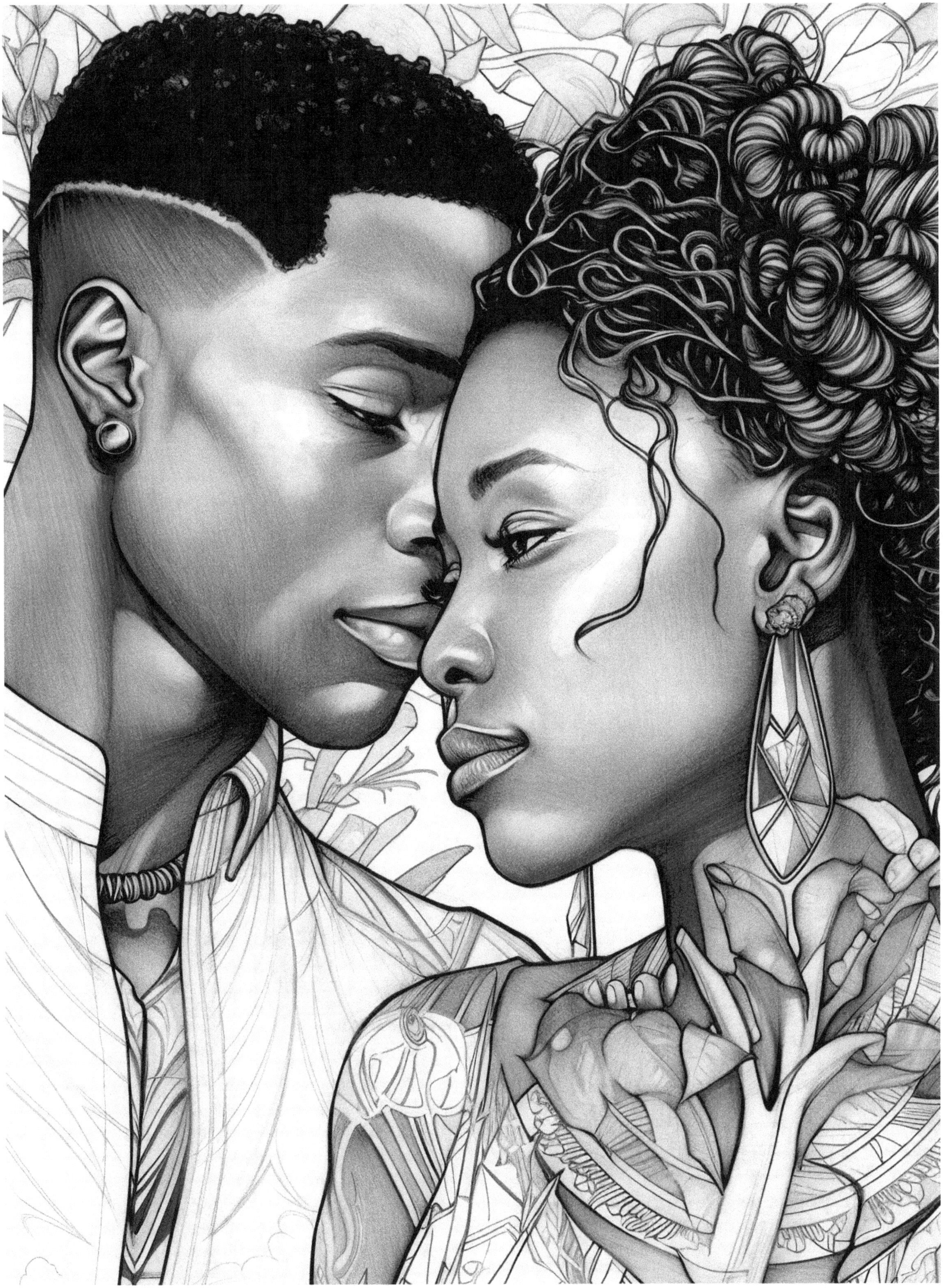

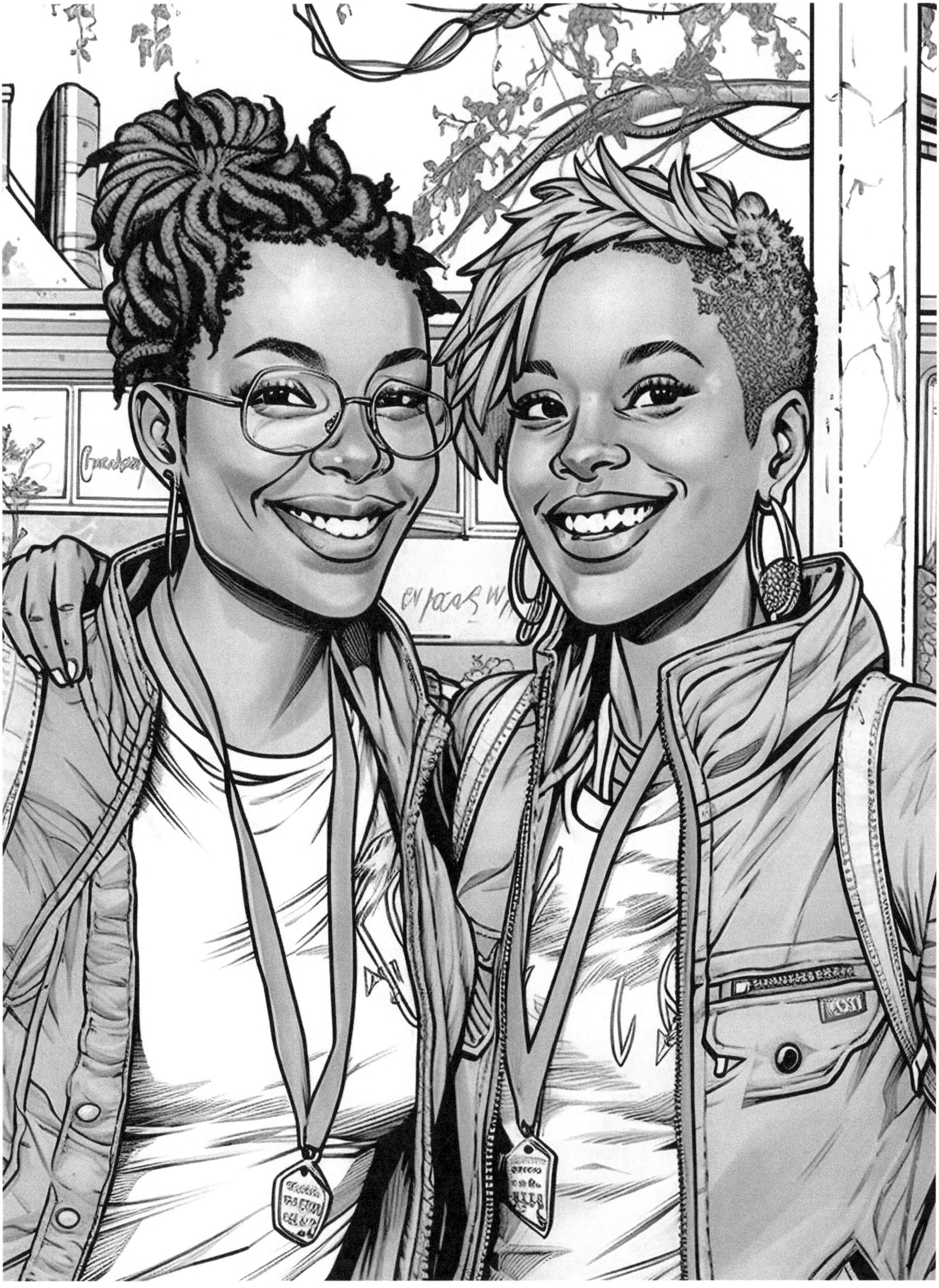

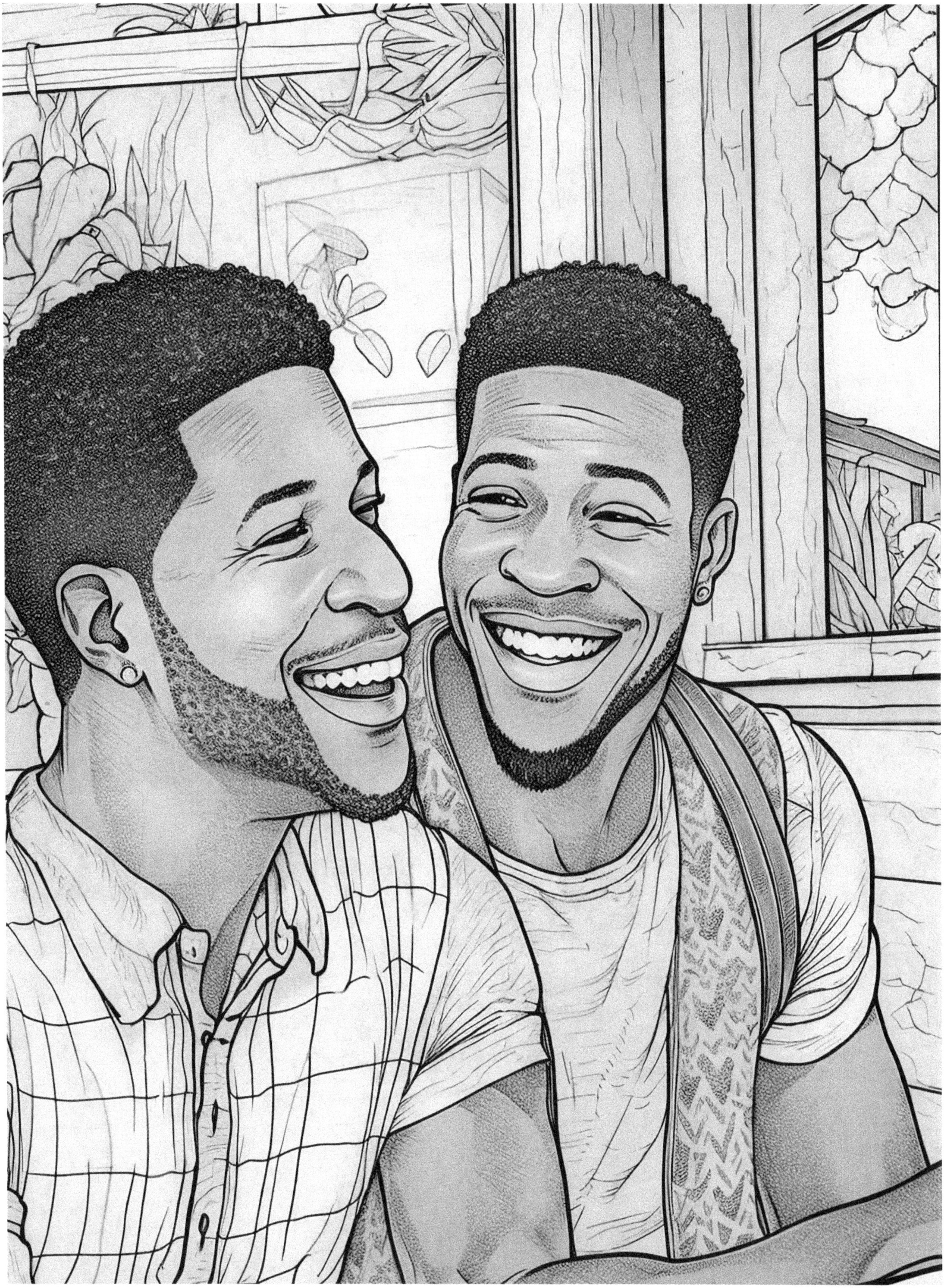

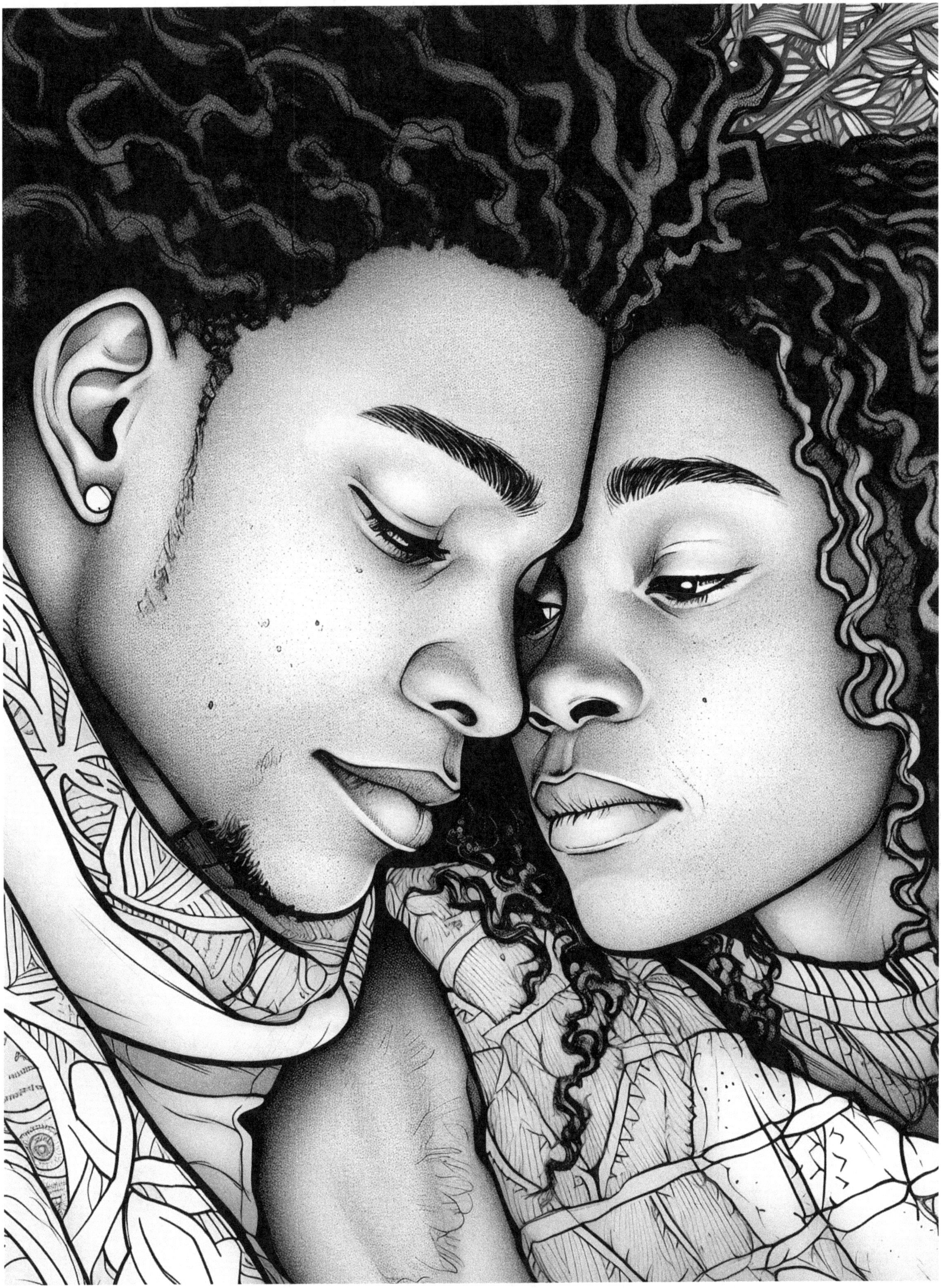

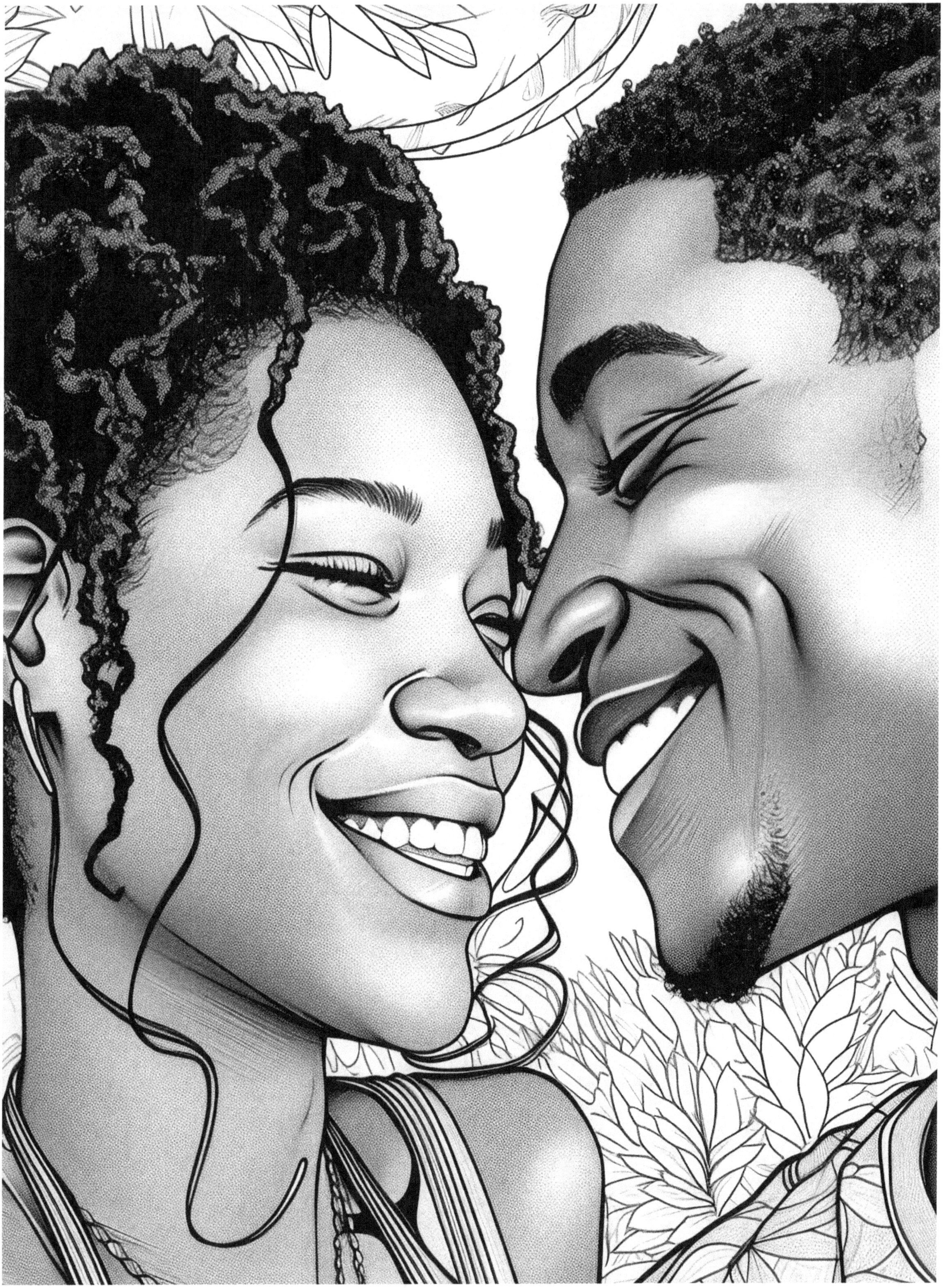

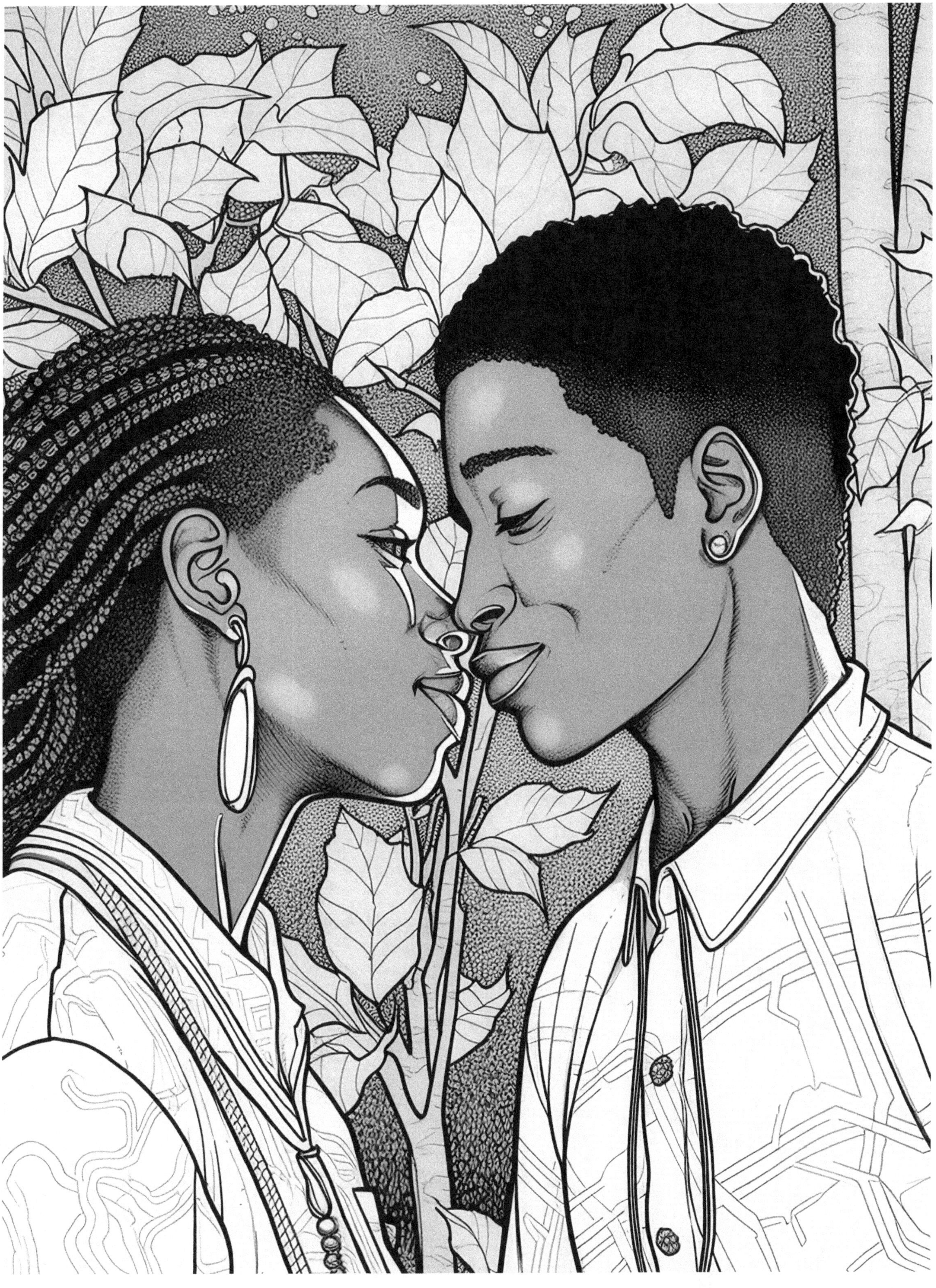

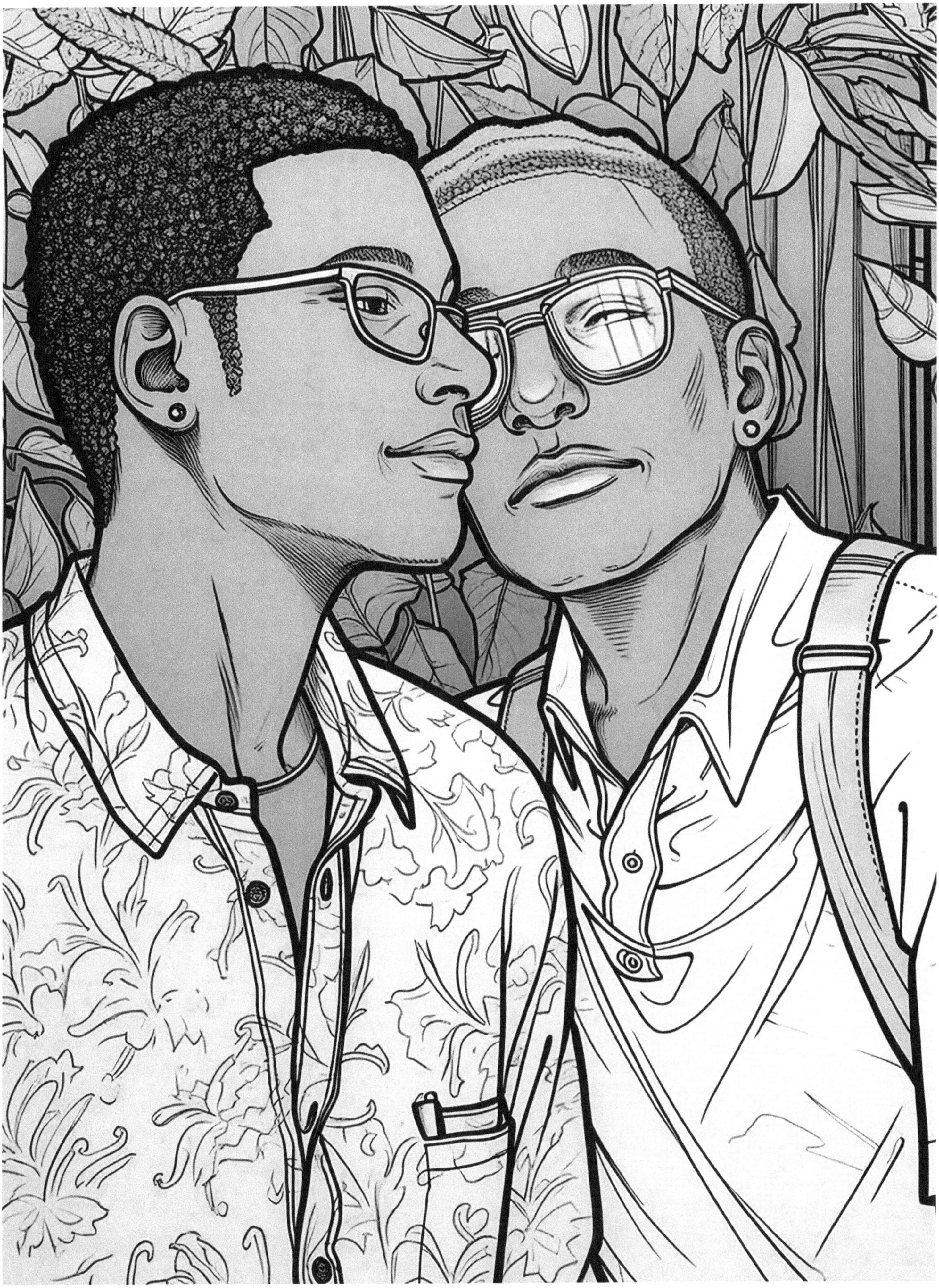

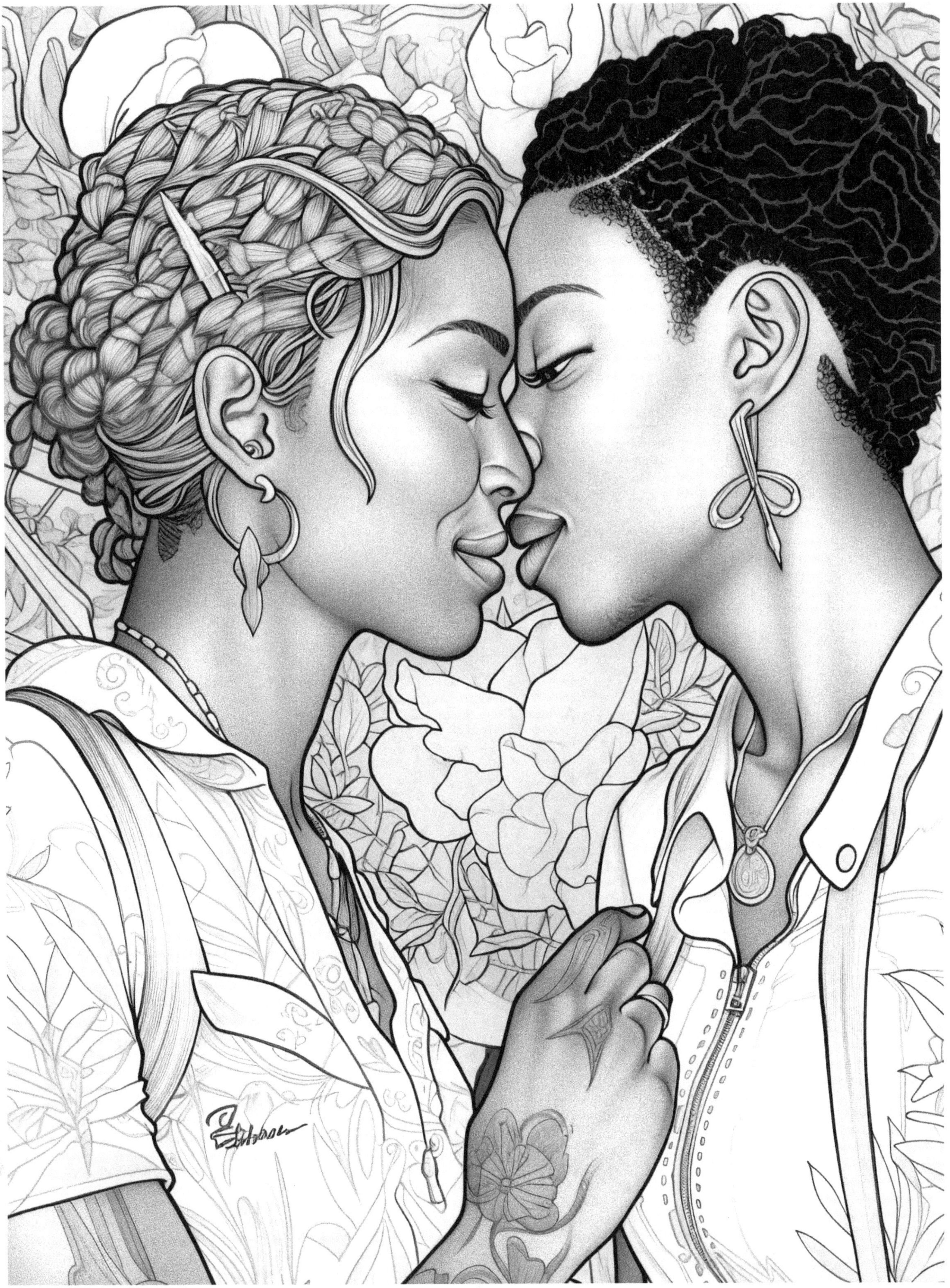

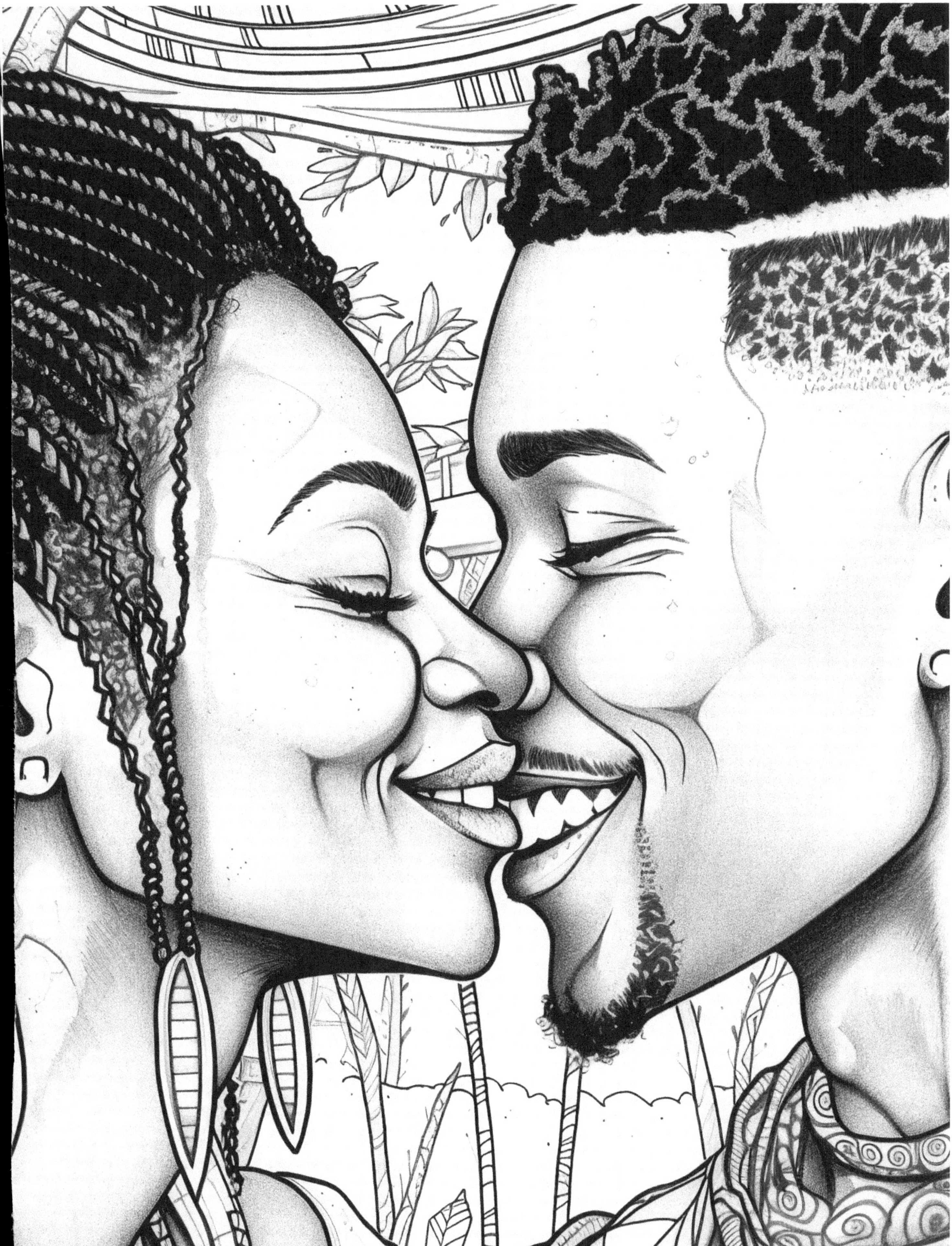

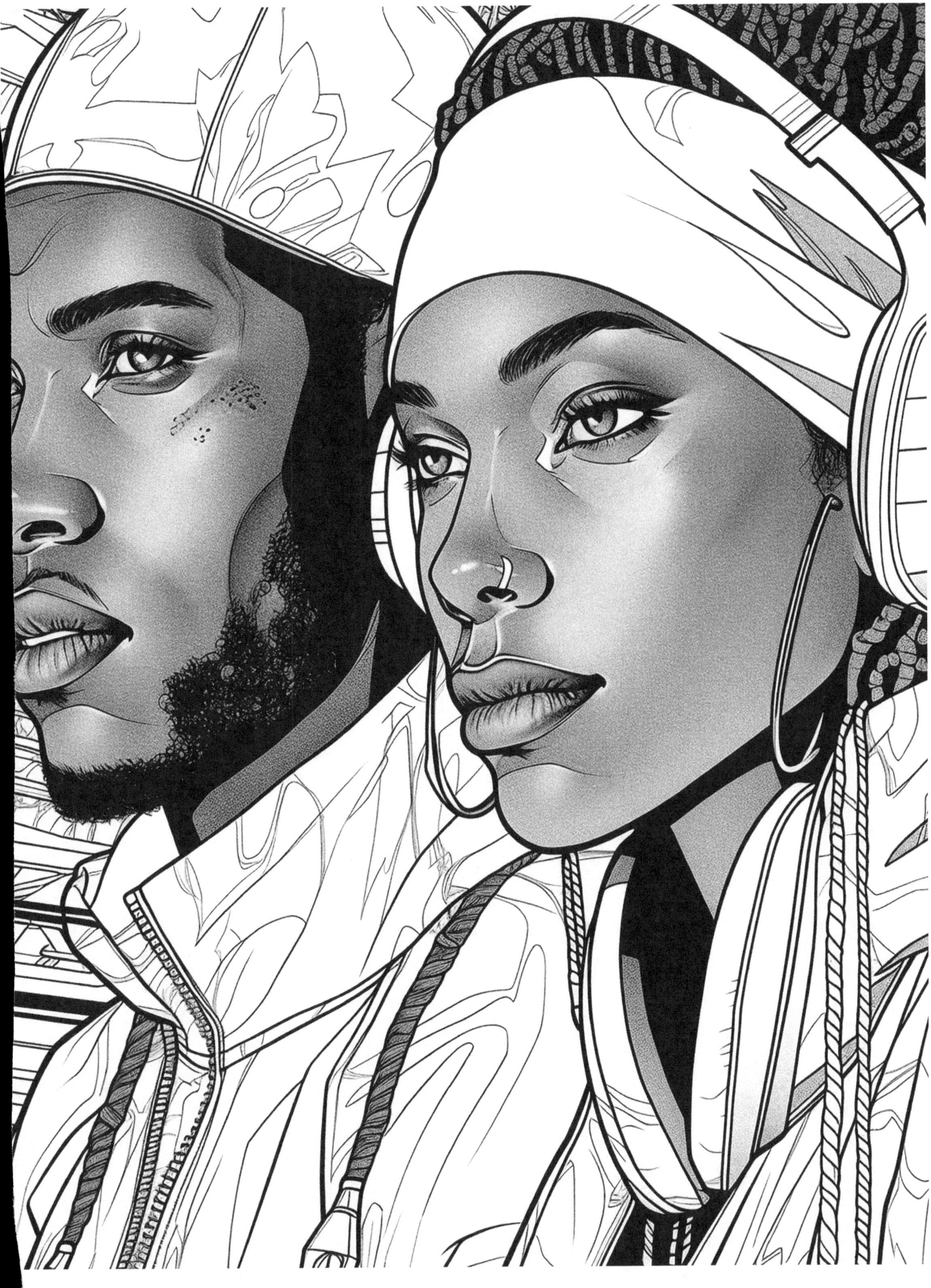

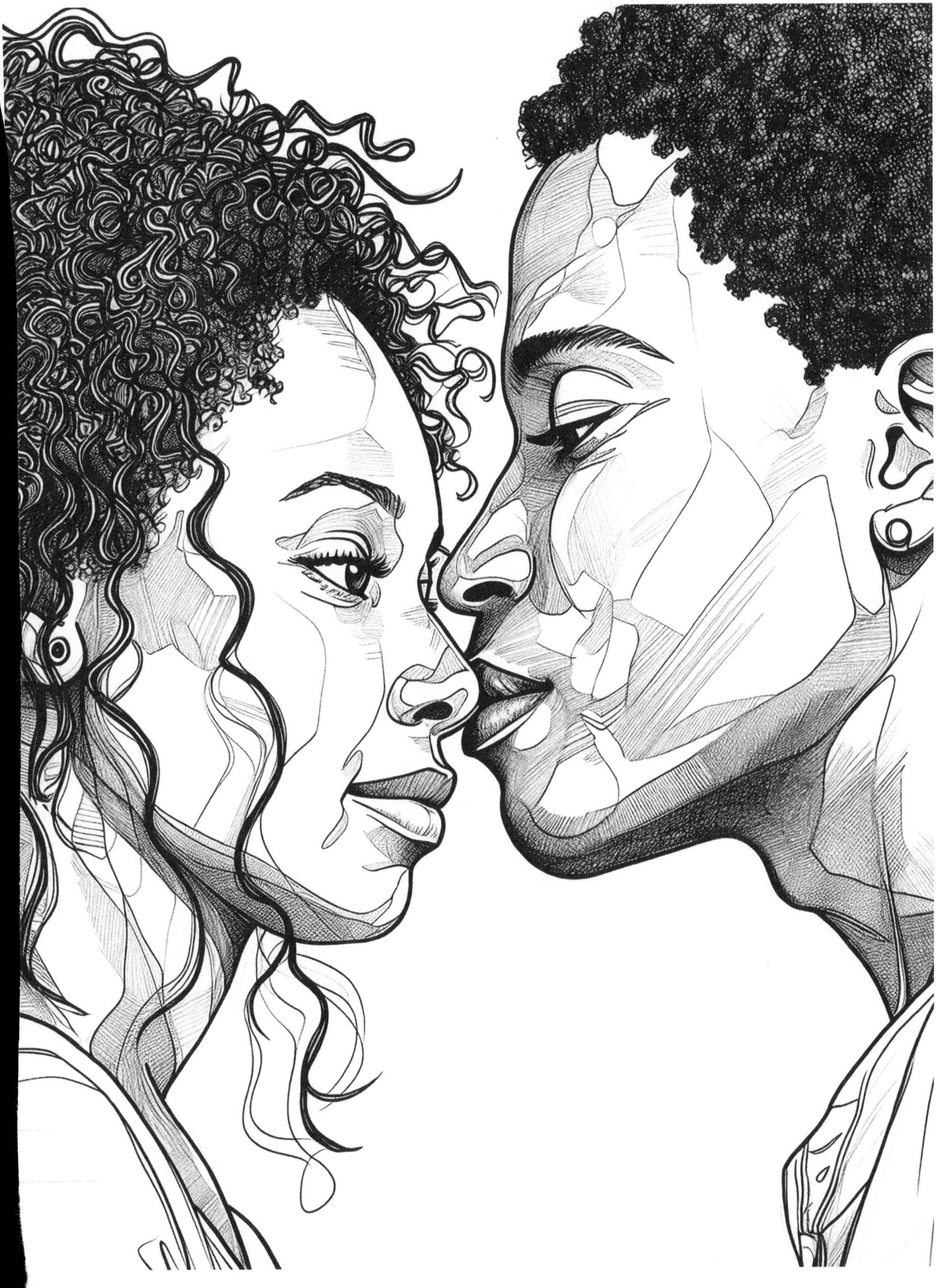

www.ingramcontent.com/pod-product-compliance
Lightning Source LLC
Chambersburg PA
CBHW082152230526
45467CB00044B/2934
* 9 7 9 8 3 9 0 1 8 7 7 1 5 *